The
Psalms
of
Mercy

The
Psalms
of
Mercy

PONTIFICAL COUNCIL FOR THE PROMOTION
OF THE NEW EVANGELIZATION

Jubilee of Mercy
2015-2016

Our Sunday Visitor Publishing Division
Our Sunday Visitor, Inc.
Huntington, Indiana 46750

Copyright © 2015 Pontifical Council for the Promotion of the New Evangelization
Vatican City

Published 2015 by Our Sunday Visitor Publishing Division

20 19 18 17 16 15   1 2 3 4 5 6 7 8 9

Our Sunday Visitor Publishing Division, Our Sunday Visitor, Inc., 200 Noll Plaza, Huntington, IN 46750; 1-800-348-2440

ISBN: 978-1-61278-976-7 (Inventory No. T1736)
eISBN: 978-1-61278-984-2
LCCN: 2015948393

Translation: Marsha Daigle-Williamson
Cover design: Lindsey Riesen
Cover art: Shutterstock; Pontifical Council for Promotion of the New Evangelization
Interior design: Sherri Hoffman

PRINTED IN THE UNITED STATES OF AMERICA

TABLE OF CONTENTS

PREFACE

The Psalms reflect everyone's life. When people approach the Psalter, whether they are believers or not, sooner or later they will find their lives reflected in these ancient poems that have become an inheritance of prayer for generations of people. Birth and death, the suffering of sickness and the pain of abandonment, war and peace, loneliness and the search for God — all these personal experiences are mirrored in the Psalms. Not just human life, but the cosmos, Israel's history, and the history of salvation find a place in the Psalms. The Psalter, in brief, is the voice of God that becomes a prayer people can use when they come into his presence knowing they need his love. It was important to offer a pastoral instrument to assist the prayer and understanding of pilgrims during the Holy Year of Mercy, so the idea arose to provide a selection of psalms in which the theme of mercy emerges with all its current relevance and theological significance.

In *Misericordiae Vultus*, Pope Francis dedicated some significant passages to the prayer of the Psalms. He wrote: "In a special way the Psalms bring to the fore the grandeur of his merciful action: 'He forgives all your iniquity, he heals all your diseases, he redeems your life from the pit, he crowns you with steadfast love and mercy' (Ps 103:3-4).... The mercy of God is not an abstract idea, but a concrete reality with which he reveals his love as of that of a father or a mother, moved to the very depths out of love for their child" (6).

The Pontifical Council for the Promotion of the New Evangelization is grateful to Father Sebastiano Pinto, professor of Old

Testament exegesis in the Theology Faculty in Puglia, for his willingness to write this commentary on *The Psalms of Mercy*. We are sure that through his presentation many Christians will appreciate and enjoy the prayer of the Psalter in a more significant way. *The Psalms of Mercy* can be a guide for a pilgrimage to the Holy Door that reveals the immanent presence of God's mercy for us, a mercy full of tenderness and consolation that is unparalleled.

✠ Rino Fisichella
President, Pontifical Council for the
Promotion of the New Evangelization

INTRODUCTION

> How I wept to hear the hymns and canticles in your honor, very moved by the voices of your church singing so sweetly! Those voices resonated in my ears, and truth was distilled in my heart. From that truth everything was transformed into emotions of love, and I was joyful as tears ran down my face. (St. Augustine, *Confessions*, 9, 6, 14).

With these impassioned words, St. Augustine describes the appeal that the Church's prayer and singing exercised in his life, together with the strong influence of liturgical song in his conversion. The Book of Psalms has always held an extraordinary attraction for people because it covers the full range of human sentiments: joy and praise, sadness and anguish, strength and weakness, victory and defeat, confidence and discouragement. Every experience in life — from the most beautiful and uplifting to the most terrible — are poetically narrated in it.

It is not without reason that St. Athanasius spoke of the Psalms as the book of the affections, as the cradle of moral life, and as the mirror of the soul because they awaken the desire for virtue (see his *Letter to Marcellinus*). Although all Scripture, old and new, is divinely inspired, this book is a rich garden, so to speak, in which we can reap fruit found in all the other inspired texts.

In the first centuries of the Church, there was a widespread Christological interpretation of the Psalms. They were considered to be not just the voice of Christ, but the voice of *Christus totus* ("the total Christ"), composed of Christ the Head and his members. We can hear Jesus' voice in David's voice, and with it the polyphony of all the members of the body of Christ. The Psalms were extensively commented on from this perspective.

If we wanted to draw up a list of commentaries on favorite biblical books by Christian authors, we would discover that the Book of Psalms is at the top along with other illustrious writings like that of the prophet Isaiah, the Song of Songs, and, of course, the Gospels. The Risen Christ, appearing to his disciples, had pointed to the Psalms not only as a place in which to trace his footsteps in this life but as the key to recognizing him as alive and at work in the Church: "Then he said to them, 'These are my words which I spoke to you, while I was still with you, that everything written about me in the law of Moses and the prophets and the psalms must be fulfilled.' Then he opened their minds to understand the Scriptures" (Lk 24:44-45).

Fascination with the Psalter has continued throughout the centuries and continues right up to our day, revealing its richness to people who have such a hunger for an inner life and the authentic meaning of life today. Its richness can be discovered in reading and studying the Psalter, whether personally or in community, but it is also found above all in the prayer of Christians in the *Liturgy of the Hours*: "In the liturgy of the hours the Church prays in large measure through the magnificent songs that the Old Testament authors composed under the inspiration of the Holy Spirit. Those who pray the psalms in the liturgy of the hours do so not so much in their own name as in the name of the entire Body of Christ" (nos. 100, 108).[1]

The Psalter is called *sefer tehillim* ("book of praises") in Hebrew, while it is called *psalmos* ("song") in Greek. In the Book of Daniel, the different musical instruments mentioned include "the horn, pipe, lyre, trigon, harp, bagpipe, and every kind of music" (3:5).

---

1. *General Instruction of the Liturgy of the Hours.* USCCB Publishing (2003), 51, 53.

The link between the Psalms and music is indissoluble according to 1 Chronicles 16:4-6 and 2 Chronicles 34:12, which present the Levites as singers and players of instruments. (This does not mean, however, that an instrument always accompanied the recitation of psalms.)

The Psalms were composed in Hebrew between the sixth and eighth centuries and were much used for prayer by the community. The Greek version of the Septuagint is the most important ancient translation of the Psalter. Written between the second century B.C. and the first century A.D., this text is significant because it is the one closest in time to the original Hebrew. It was this Greek text rather than the Hebrew text that was cited by the authors of the New Testament whenever they referred to the Old Testament. The same is true for the Fathers of the Church, who also used this version of the Psalter. The most widespread circulation of the Psalter, however, occurred in its Latin translation; in 386 in Bethlehem, St. Jerome finished the *Psalterium Gallicanum* that then became the Psalter for the Vulgate version of the Bible.

In perusing the different psalms the reader becomes aware that the majority of them include inscriptions at the top that serve as their titles or headings. These headings did not appear in the original Hebrew, although their antiquity is indisputable. These headers were inserted by the pre-Christian Hebrew tradition for important liturgical reasons. There are three types of headings: a) technical words about the music with indications for the psalm's performance, b) personal names the psalm is associated with, and c) historical captions.

Looking through the Psalter, a reader may find it difficult to know a psalm's exact number because beginning with Psalm 9 there is a dual enumeration. The Hebrew text considers the second half of Psalm 9 as Psalm 10 while the Septuagint and the Vulgate do not divide Psalm 9. Therefore, starting with Psalm 9 a double numbering is included by many modern translations of the Bible. The higher number (usually in parentheses) comes from the Hebrew text while the lower number follows the ordering in the Septuagint and the Vulgate. The dual numbering stops at Psalm 147, where we find the exact reverse of what occurred with Psalm 9. The Hebrew text separates Psalm 147 into Psalm 146 and 147, which explains why both the Hebrew and Greek Bibles have a total of 150 psalms in the end. (We should keep in mind, however, that the division of the Hebrew Bible into chapters and verses came much later between the fourth and seventh centuries.)

The Psalter has always been considered a book in itself, although the final editors of the Bible gave it its unity. Exegetical commentaries, however, often prefer to deal with individual poems and do not note the internal links within the book. Another legitimate approach, especially in recent decades, has developed more awareness of these links and treats individual poems together, grouping them according to a common theme. According to St. Gregory of Nyssa's analysis, some elements in the Psalter allow us to organize it into five books: 1-41, the first book; 42-72, the second book; 73-89, the third book; 90-106, the fourth book; and 107-150, the fifth book.

The presence of five books demonstrates the final editors' wishes to parallel the Psalter with the first five books of the Bible, the Pentateuch, conferring on it an analogous established value. Just as the Pentateuch narrates the beginnings of the history of salvation (creation, election, slavery, liberation, the gift of the law), so, too, the Psalter outlines the itinerary of the spiritual journey of a devout Israelite. The praise that ends each of the five books — and the entirely doxological hymn of Psalm 150 — demonstrates the conclusion that the Psalms lead to: despite ordeals, unfaithfulness, and the sins of individuals and of the people as a whole, the promise of the Lord remains unshakable, assuring the Israelites of recovery of health for the body and spiritual communion for the spirit.

We normally think that the natural context for the Psalms is the Temple in Jerusalem, or at least an environment connected to the study of Scripture in the synagogue. However, the places in which the compositions were celebrated (and certainly revised) do not need to be combined with the contexts that sparked their poetic and spiritual inspiration. The Psalms come out of daily life and, therefore, intend to express all of life's seasons poetically, whether those seasons are green and fruitful or yellowed and withered. The Psalms are poems with a religious theme, and to understand them deeply calls for the dual competence of a poetic sensibility that can discern the nuances of the Hebrew poetry and a faith that can understand their spiritual value.

The Psalter, in short, speaks about human beings, which explains the unlimited richness of its symbols. According to a description that has now become famous, the 150 psalms constitute a "microcosm" that encloses the entire space-time continuum of human beings understood in their psychological-physical unity. Human beings are spirit, heart, and imagination, and when they think about God and live out their faith, they do so with their whole being; they cannot be considered only in terms of reason, intellect, or a cold algebraic sum of variables. The symbols in the Psalms play a major role because they express the "flavor" of theology and, in the last analysis, the "flavor" of existence.

There are three fundamental categories that describe human beings symbolically. The first is *vertical*: "a person standing up" in an ascending-descending line during the process of moral and social elevation. In this category we find the symbol of the scepter or rod (see Ps 2:9; 45:6; 60:7; 108:8), the slave who lifts his eyes to his master (123:1-2), and references to the divine names of the Lord on high, the mighty Lord on high, and the Lord in heaven (see, respectively, 92:8; 93:4; 102:19).

The second category is *horizontal*: "a seated person" as a sign of intimacy. We can think of references that use the verbs "to inhabit, dwell, lie down (*yasab*)" and speak of dwelling places: the home (see Ps 26:8; 84:4; 101:7; 113:9), the temple (11:4; 27:4; 65:4), and the city of refuge (62:7-8; 144:2).

Finally, the third category is *dynamic* and *temporal*: "a person on his or her journey." Here the dominant image of the path (*derek*) indicates a road but also moral conduct. The image of "two paths" concerns good in contrast to evil. This is not, therefore, just a geographical symbol but also a symbol of life or a life orientation (see Ps 49:10-14; 119). The movement can be ascending (up toward the temple in Psalms 120-134), or linked to the passage of time (16:10-11).

In terms of spatial symbolism, we can say that the Psalms follow four tracks: *vertical-theological*, toward heaven and God; *horizontal-anthropological*, toward human beings; *horizontal-cosmological*, toward creation; and *vertical in the afterlife*, toward the world of darkness that the Hebrew imagination locates under the earth.

The Ten Psalms of Mercy

Mercy is one of God's most highlighted characteristics in the Psalter. There are, in fact, poems that we can call "the Psalms of Mercy" because they are filled with the loving action of the Lord toward his faithful. The word "mercy" (*hesed*) has many significant meanings, so it is translated in a variety of ways, as "tenderness, grace, mercy, forgiveness, goodness, benevolence, steadfast love." These words reveal a surprising feature about God: motherhood. If there is a place in which divine *hesed* dwells, it is the womb, the viscera (*rahamim*). We see God's "maternal viscera" activated to the point of forgiving great sins (see Is 49:15; Ps 103:13). In the biblical world the most intimate part in which sentiments are located is the belly, the womb, creating a strong link between mercy and physical generation. "To bring forth mercy" is the equivalent of "to bring life into the world."

The Psalms give voice to human beings and their bodies: it is precisely through the body and its members that prayer finds its modulations, its rhythms, its seasons. It is not the case that the soul and spirit are uninvolved, but the Bible has a "carnal" conception of man in the most spiritual sense of that word: a body is not considered separately from the soul, and a soul is not considered in detachment from its body. When people pray, love, suffer, praise — in a word, when they live — they do so with their whole psychophysical beings. Perhaps a certain Christian vision has lingered too much and for too long on only the rational dimension of a human being, consigning the physical to a secondary status, which can lead people to think that the noblest form of prayer is the prayer of the mind. However, due to a reassessment by biblical anthropology, the "flesh of faith" has been put at the center, and with it the existential depth that runs through the great stories of the Bible from Abraham to Jesus Christ.

The Psalms give voice to the body, or, to recall a famous expression by Paul Beauchamp, they are the prayer of the body. According to him, the body is the delicate instrument of prayer, the most sensitive harp, at times the most slender block or obstacle to the soul's penchant to wickedness. It seems that for the psalmist everything is played out there, in the body. He is not indifferent to the soul, but the soul does not express itself except with the body. Meditation is externalized whenever the words "murmur or whisper" and "sigh" appear.[2] The body is the dwelling place of the soul, so prayer concerns everything in the body. Even the body itself prays: "All my bones shall say, / 'O Lord, who is like you?' " (Ps 35:10).

This presentation of the Psalms of Mercy — the most significant psalms linked to mercy in the Psalter's five books — will focus much attention on this body-soul unity. This rich anthropology not only does justice to the biblical vision of the human being, but also respects the manner in which God has decided to make himself known. God speaks a language that can be understood by everyone, and he speaks to everyone as a friend (see *Dei Verbum*, 2).

---

2. See Paul Beauchamp, *Psaumes nuit et jour* (Paris: Editions du Seuil, 1980).

Psalm 25

Aleph [1]To you, O LORD, I lift up my soul.
Beth [2]O my God, in you I trust,
  let me not be put to shame;
  let not my enemies exult over me.
Gimel [3]Yes, let none that wait for you be put to shame;
  let them be ashamed who are wantonly treacherous.

Daleth [4]Make me to know your ways, O LORD;
  teach me your paths.
He [5]Lead me in your truth, and teach me,
  for you are the God of my salvation;
Waw for you I wait all the day long.

Zayin [6]Be mindful of your compassion, O LORD,
   and of your merciful love,
  for they have been from of old.
Heth [7]Remember not the sins of my youth,
   or my transgressions;
  according to your mercy remember me,
  for your goodness' sake, O LORD!

Teth [8]Good and upright is the LORD;
  therefore he instructs sinners in the way.

Yod [9]He leads the humble in what is right,
    and teaches the humble his way.
Kaph [10]All the paths of the LORD are mercy
        and faithfulness,
    for those who keep his covenant and his testimonies.

Lamed [11]For your name's sake, O LORD,
    pardon my guilt, for it is great.
Mem [12]Who is the man that fears the LORD?
    Him will he instruct in the way that he
        should choose.
Nun [13]He himself shall abide in prosperity,
    and his children shall possess the land.
Samek [14]The friendship of the LORD is for those
        who fear him,
    and he makes known to them his covenant.
Ayin [15] My eyes are ever toward the LORD,
    for he will pluck my feet out of the net.

Pe [16]Turn to me, and be gracious to me;
    for I am lonely and afflicted.
Sadeh [17]Relieve the troubles of my heart,
    and bring me out of my distresses.
Qoph [18]Consider my affliction and my trouble,
    and forgive all my sins.

Resh [19] Consider how many are my foes,
    and with what violent hatred they hate me.
Shin [20] Oh, guard my life, and deliver me;
    let me not be put to shame, for I take refuge in you.
Taw [21]May integrity and uprightness preserve me,
    for I wait for you.

[22] Redeem Israel, O God,
    out of all his troubles.

The structure of Psalm 25 is based on the Hebrew alphabet. This composition (alphabetical acrostic) is found in other psalms as well. It has a mnemonic function and is meant to encompass the totality of a person's inner experience. The poem is presented as an individual supplication: the man praying feels oppressed by his enemies and turns to God in a confident way to free him from this situation. In addition, the psalm presents a structure whose rhythmic quality points to the poem's theme as being "the path."

v. 1. This initial antiphon records the attitude of the man who is praying; it is as if he is aiming to lift up his soul, just as we pray at Mass, "Let us lift up our hearts." The soul (*nephesh*) is a word whose meaning comes from the way it sounds. Its first meaning is "throat," through which air passes, so it means "breath" and, ultimately, the yearning of a human being, the part of a person that desires. The biblical vision of a human being is never presented as a dichotomy (the spiritual part as opposed to the physical) but as a unity. Here that word points to the very life of a human being, and the psalmist is praying with his whole being as he desires to be lifted up and reach the divine sphere spiritually.

vv. 2-3. Trust, hope, and shame. The psalmist professes his trust in God, beseeching him not to be put to shame. The reasons for his hope are not ultimately found in these verses, but they run throughout the entire poem. In this initial stanza he expresses unconditional trust in God.

What does the psalmist fear? From whom and from what does he want to be freed? Verse 2 speaks of "enemies" while verse 3 speaks of the "treacherous." The phrase "wantonly treacherous" (or "to betray without reason") could recall vocabulary related to the covenant that speaks about the sin of idolatry (see Ps 78:57-58; Hos 6:7; Mal 2:11). The concepts of futility and frustration are often connected specifically to gods that have no substance because they do not exist: "They have mouths, but do not speak.... / They have ears, but do not hear.... / They have ... feet, but do not walk" (Ps 115:5-7). The psalmist puts all his trust in God, knowing that he has expressed his feelings to the God who hears, and he desires that his enemies and the treacherous instead experience frustration.

vv. 4-7. "Lead me.... Be mindful." There is an abundance of words related to the road, the path, the way, and the steps to take, as if his clear request, in imperative verb forms, is for God to be his light and guide. The paths he refers to are metaphors for the moral conduct the man wants to learn directly from God ("Make me to know your ways ... your paths," v. 4). The theme of the two paths (the paths of good and evil) is typical of the Wisdom tradition (see Prv 2 and 9) and is often found in the Psalter. The so-called portal to the Book of Psalms — Psalms 1 and 2 — revolves around the idea that the person who follows the way of the Lord, meditating on his law and avoiding the paths of the wicked, will have a prosperous and happy life; on the other hand, the person who follows evil will be swept away by the wind like chaff. The reference to training in verse 5 ("teach me") is also typical of the Wisdom tradition. In the school of Wisdom the disciple learns the art of journeying uprightly, and above all he acquires the discernment necessary to avoid the footsteps of the wicked and being bewitched by their enticing proposals (Prv 1:18-19; 2:12-13,15).

In verses 6-7, with more imperative verbs ("Be mindful.... Remember not"), the man praying appeals directly to God's mercy and goodness. It seems somewhat odd that God has to be urged to remember his qualities by this man's prayer, but we need to bear in mind that such calls are typical in supplications. The prayer of Ezra the scribe occurs, for example, in the continuum of the history of salvation, and his recalling of past divine miracles (anamnesis) is preparation for an invocation in the "here and now" (epiclesis) that anticipates God's future presence, which he waits for with trust and surrender (see Ezr 9).

As for compassion (*rahamin*) and merciful love (*hesed*), in verse 6, as already noted, the Lord acts with a maternal womb and knows how to love with the same intensity that a woman loves her own child. This kind of mercy characterizes the intimacy of God's action and is a characteristic "from of old" (v. 6), a characteristic written into God's DNA, so to speak. The same point is made in Psalm 78, a long meditation on the people's sin and divine forgiveness:

> Yet he, being compassionate,
>   forgave their iniquity,
>   and did not destroy them;
> he restrained his anger often,
>   and did not stir up all his wrath.
> He remembered that they were but flesh,
>   a wind that passes and comes not again.
> How often they rebelled against him in the wilderness
>   and grieved him in the desert!" (vv. 38-40)

In Psalm 25 we are seeing a kind of inversion of roles. Although God remains the teacher, it is also true that the man praying knows exactly what he is requesting, and that leads him to "instruct" the Lord about what to do: "Remember not the sins of my youth, or my transgressions" (v. 7). The effect of this inversion of roles is to bring him a greater consciousness of his own sin in the face of God's mercy.

The psalmist, now elderly, knows his state of serious transgression. The first word he uses for "sin" is *hatta't* in Hebrew. Because of its vague, generic nature, this word is used in the Bible for sin more than any other word (595 times). Etymologically it suggests the idea of missing or failing to hit the mark (*hamartia* in Greek). Its metaphoric meaning refers to a failure to reach a moral and religious goal. The person who commits *hatta't* is not following the right trajectory, is wandering, is moving away from reaching the objective. The men from the tribe of Benjamin were able to sling a stone at a hair without missing (see Jdg 20:16), but the sinner does not even come close to the target.

The second word he uses, "transgression," is *pesha'*, and it has a wide range of meanings. The prophet Amos, in his oracles against the nations, specifies the list of sins connected to this noun: political crimes that are not pleasing to the Lord tied to the covenant and the deportation of the masses, violence against the weak, disdain for the law of God in profaning the temple, disdain for him in appropriating for themselves the offerings meant for the Temple, and practices that make people unclean. The word *pesha'* concerns social sins or sins of unfaithfulness to God.

vv. 8–11. The path of the covenant. The heart of this psalm is presented in vv. 8-11 and 12-15 (B and B'). The themes of the path and the covenant constitute the specific features of this stanza (see also Ps 119). The qualities that belong to God are repeated in a rapid, pounding fashion (goodness, uprightness, mercy, faithfulness). The concept of God as the teacher is reiterated in verses 8-9, and the request for forgiveness reoccurs in verse 11. The disciples the Lord addresses his teachings to are the "sinners" and the "humble." The first word is *hatta't*, and we already spoke of its meaning as "one who misses the goal." The second word is *'anawim* and indicates the poor from the material point of view (Prv 14:21; Am 2:7). Extrapolating from that primary meaning, the psalmist uses that word here to refer to those who are conscious of their lowly status and weakness and place their trust only in God (Ps 69:33; Is 29:19; Lk 6:20).

The meaning of verse 2 now becomes clearer. The psalmist is placing himself in the group of the humble who wait on God for everything and are conscious of their state of sin ("pardon my guilt," v. 11).

The topic of the covenant is central for the psalmist because he knows that divine mercy is linked to respect for the covenant. The word *berit* has a primary and immediate reference to an alliance between two parties who "cut" a covenant (*karat berit*), stipulating an agreement by dividing an animal in two. The two parties walk through the middle of the animal's body, committing themselves reciprocally to observe what was agreed to and pledging that the same fate of the animal will befall them if they do not respect the pact. In Genesis 15 there is a very important passage that refers to this practice. God invites Abraham to split animals in two but *only God*, however, walks through the middle of the animals, thereby signifying his assumption of an obligation and commitment in which he is the *only* guarantor of this covenant (a unilateral covenant). In contrast, in Exodus 19-20 there is a bilateral covenant in which Israel will have a special relationship with YHWH but must obey the Decalogue. This second covenant is the one the psalm refers to here. The man who is praying is very aware of his own sin but opens himself up like the "little ones," trusting in God's mercy and expecting forgiveness.

vv. 12-15. B', The path of the covenant and fear of the Lord. The themes of the fear of the Lord and the covenant return now. The reflection moves between the traditional theological coordinates that link faithfulness to God to well-being ("prosperity, and his children," v. 13). We recalled the theme of just rewards above on the basis of which a faithful person enjoys the sign of blessing through earthly goods. Wealth, offspring, and land are, therefore, God's gifts for the one who observes the covenant, together with the knowledge of the mystery of God and the protection he gives to his friends (who frees them like a bird from the net of the fowler; see Ps 31:4; Prv 6:5).

The statement that "the friendship of the LORD is for those who fear him" in verse 14 can be explained by recalling a beautiful passage in Genesis 18. In Hebrew, *sod* is the advice or secret someone shares with an intimate friend (see Prv 25:9). In the account of Sodom and Gomorrah, the Lord lets Abraham know of his plan to destroy the city:

> The LORD said, "Shall I hide from Abraham what I am about to do, seeing that Abraham shall become a great and mighty nation, and all the nations of the earth shall bless themselves by him?..." Then the LORD said, "Because the outcry against Sodom and Gomorrah is great and their sin is very grave, I will go down to see

whether they have done altogether according to the out-
cry which has come to me; and if not, I will know."

Then Abraham drew near, and said, "Will you indeed
destroy the righteous with the wicked?" (Gn 18:17-21,23)

A friendly negotiation begins between God and Abraham concerning the salvation of the city if at least ten righteous people could
be found there. We can say, then, the psalmist declares that the
covenant makes the Lord an intimate friend of his faithful one and
does not want to hide anything from him.

Finally, a comment on the topic of "land" (v. 13). It is indisputable that originally that word referred to the land of Canaan, the
Promised Land (see Gn 24:5-6; Dt 26:9; Jos 24:2-13). However,
during the course of theological reflection, this word underwent a
process of spiritualization, and "land" began to refer to something
not so narrowly restricted to the boundaries of Israel. The "land"
came to signify the fullness of life the Lord gives in this world (Prv
2:21-22) as well as life in the world to come (Mt 5:5).

*vv. 16-19. A', "Turn to me ... bring me out of my distresses ... for-
give."* The prayer moves to a direct invocation of God and his mercy.
The psalmist's supplication wants to draw attention to his doubly
miserable condition. He is, in fact, completely immersed in sin
(that is the case throughout the whole poem), but he is also alone
and defenseless before his enemies. Earlier, verses 2-3 mentioned
enemies and traitors, and we now learn that his foes are numerous
and accustomed to committing evil. The phrase "with what violent
hatred they hate me" (v. 19) literally means they hate him with "the
hatred of violence," a repetition that provokes a redundant effect in
portraying these enemies as intrinsically evil.

Nevertheless, if we look carefully, what emerges is that the most
anguishing reality for the psalmist seems to be his sin. Although it
is true that he has an external enemy, it is just as true that his inner
condition of the absence of God's grace causes him much more fear.
His worst anguish comes from seeing his own sin (see Ps 51).

vv. 20-21. Trust, hope, and shame. These topics were already linked at the beginning in verses 2 and 3. At the end of the psalm the state of this man's soul surfaces again, but this time with a difference. This elderly man has openly declared his own condition, but now, with great confidence, he opens himself up to receive God's mercy in the expectation of forgiveness. Disclosing one's sin is, in fact, the precondition for obtaining pardon (see Ps 51:4).

v. 22. This final verse is a rereading of the psalm by the postexilic community. It is significant to note the enormous adaptability of the psalms as prayers. The community accepts and receives the cry of the suffering person and experiences it as resonating with their own situation. The perspective of an individual person is replaced by a wider faith context with respect to his initial situation. The psalm is thus enriched because a more profound and ecclesial spiritual tenor has been conferred on it.

Psalm 41

To the choirmaster.
A Psalm of David.

[1]Blessed is he who considers the poor!
    The Lord delivers him in the day of trouble;
[2]the Lord protects him and keeps him alive;
    he is called blessed in the land;
    you do not give him up to the will of his enemies.
[3]The Lord sustains him on his sickbed;
    in his illness you heal all his infirmities.

[4]As for me, I said, "O Lord, be gracious to me;
    heal me, for I have sinned against you!"
[5]My enemies say of me in malice:
    "When will he die, and his name perish?"
[6]And when one comes to see me, he utters empty words.
    while his heart gathers mischief.
    When he goes out, he tells it abroad.
[7]All who hate me whisper together about me;
    they imagine the worst for me.

[8]They say, "A deadly thing has fastened upon him;
    he will not rise again from where he lies."
[9]Even my bosom friend in whom I trusted,
    who ate of my bread, has lifted his heel against me.

¹⁰But you, O Lord, be gracious to me,
>   and raise me up, that I may repay them!

¹¹By this I know that you are pleased with me,
>   in that my enemy has not triumphed over me.
¹²But you have upheld me because of my integrity,
>   and set me in your presence for ever.

¹³Blessed be the Lord, the God of Israel,
>   from everlasting to everlasting!
>   Amen and amen.

The tone of the supplicant dominates in this psalm; a sick person turns to the Lord to be freed of his infirmity with a solid assurance his prayer will be heard because the Lord is merciful. The heading for this composition is very generic: "To the choirmaster. A Psalm of David." It does not allow us to connect the psalm to any particular historical situation.

We can subdivide the poem into three parts: the wisdom hymn (vv. 1-4), a lament against his enemies (vv. 5-9), and a profession of faith (vv. 10-12). It ends with a community rereading in verse 13.

vv. 1-3. The wisdom hymn. "Blessed is he [or the man] ... " is a statement that characterizes various psalms (see 32:1-2; 112:1; 127:5). It introduces the Psalter I (Ps 1:1) and characterizes the people who approach the Lord with trust: they will be happy because they will enjoy special protection from the Lord who will not abandon them and, in addition, will sustain them especially in their most difficult moments. The "portal" to the Psalter (Psalms 1 and 2) presents the theme of beatitude that marks the whole book. In the joyful or sorrowful events within the whole range of situations presented by the various poems, beatitude is reserved to the faithful who love God and are in solidarity with their neighbor.

Psalm 41 praises the attitude of compassion: "Blessed is he who considers the poor!" (v. 1). The logic of the verse is that if someone draws near to a human being who is in difficulty, like a poor person (the word *dal* means materially poor; see Am 2:7) — or a weak and oppressed person in general — he or she will receive the same treatment. The first stanza can be called a "Wisdom hymn," because it is full of instruction by Israel's teachers regarding charity toward one's neighbor. If people help a brother or sister, they will be helped in turn in their moment of need: "He who closes his ear to the cry of the poor / will himself cry out and not be heard" (Prv 21:13). In looking closely at the Wisdom tradition, one becomes aware that reasons for this charity go beyond the simple reciprocity of quid pro quo (*do ut des*) because an action on behalf of the oppressed has a theological dimension: "He who is kind to the poor lends to the LORD, / and he will repay him for his deed" (Prv 19:17), and again, "He who oppresses a poor man insults his Maker, / but he who is kind to the needy honors him" (Prv 14:31).

Verses 2-3 of Psalm 41 thus present the logic for uniting the love of God and love of neighbor, the same logic Jesus uses in his teaching (see Mt 22:36-40; Lk 10:25-27).

vv. 4-9. A lament against enemies. The approach that we call "remunerative" is very ingrained in biblical thinking. It is a logic in which sickness is a sign of sin, and the more chronic it is the more serious the transgression that was committed. The connection between offense-punishment is present as the psalmist invokes divine forgiveness for himself. In admitting his sin, he is thus expecting his healing.

Verses 5-9 recall a similar event for Job when he finds himself poor and afflicted with leprosy. His friends ask him to acknowledge his sin so he can receive healing; they think he should in some way "negotiate" for a lessening of his pain. Eliphaz, one of Job's three friends who come visit him after they hear about his illness, approaches him, saying:

"As for me, I would seek God,
    and to God would I commit my cause;

who does great things and unsearchable,
    marvelous things without number:
he gives rain upon the earth
    and sends waters upon the fields;
he sets on high those who are lowly,
    and those who mourn are lifted to safety.
He frustrates the devices of the crafty,
    so that their hands achieve no success.

"Behold, happy is the man whom God reproves;
    therefore despise not the chastening of the Almighty.
For he wounds, but he binds up;
    he strikes, but his hands heal." (Jb 5:8-12,17-18)

Although Job does not follow his friend's advice, the psalmist does offer an act of repentance. He seems less preoccupied with divine punishment, insofar as he trusts in God, than with the presence of his enemies. We can almost imagine the scene: presumptuous friends (or at least acquaintances) visit the sick man and, instead of wishing him well and wishing him a speedy recovery, they wish death for him. Their bad intentions make their visit particularly unpleasant, and, in addition, in leaving the sick man's house they slander him (see vv. 6-7).

What can account for their falseness? Why so much hate? Verse 8 reports one of the things said by the false friends: "A deadly thing has fastened upon him; / he will not rise again from where he lies." The "deadly thing" here is literally "something of Belial." "Belial" can mean "something good for nothing," although rabbinical usage understood it to be a kind of personification of Belial, an evil demon (see 2 Cor 6:15: "What accord has Christ with Belial? Or what has a believer in common with an unbeliever?"). The combination of sickness and the presence of a demonic being also occurs at the beginning of the Book of Job, when Satan is the one who provokes his misfortunes (Chapters 1-2); it is also found in Tobit when the demon Asmodeus makes it impossible for Sarah to have a husband (Tb 3:8,17). The psalmist makes that connection in his case because it creates a heightened effect (obviously a negative one). His sickness has something superhuman, something unbearable, about it. Its seriousness is not common but "extraordinary," and thus the sin that caused it has something demonic about it too.

What can explain the malice of the "friends"? There is no answer to that question. Gratuitous pleasure in the misfortunes of others remains a mystery. We can only hypothesize that when people follow a theology of punishment in which sickness is the punishment for sin, they sternly blame the suffering person.

The practice of visiting the sick is mentioned in the Bible (see 2 Sm 13:5-6; 2 Kgs 8:29; Jb 2:11-13; Jas 5:14). That makes the content of verse 9 particularly sad: "Even my bosom friend in whom I trusted, / who ate of my bread, has lifted his heel against me." When a friend is a betrayer (like Judas was to Jesus), it always causes a mixture of surprise and disappointment. Intimate actions such as eating together are recalled with particular anguish in the light of the new situation of abandonment. The Book of Proverbs states a somewhat uncomfortable truth that can help us interpret this psalm: "The poor is disliked even by his neighbor, / but the rich has many friends" (Prv 14:20). The "poor" here can mean either an unfortunate person or a sick person. The psalmist would expect some kind of support from his friend, since true friendship is measured in misfortune (Prv 17:17; 27:10). Instead, his friend's inexplicable hostility makes his sickness ultimately more painful.

vv. 10–12. Profession of faith. Verse 10 uses the verb "be gracious" (*hanan*), the verb for compassion and mercy already used in verse 4. The psalmist has full faith in God because he is sure of being freed from his ignominious condition. We are still in the realm of "remunerative" logic — "that I may repay them!" — in which God's justice is invoked for the ruin of his enemies. His logic, though, is inspired by a desire for truth. Since his false friends put his integrity in doubt — in their limited perspective he deserves evil — this sick person asks for justice and wants to be officially acknowledged in his new condition of physical and moral health. Sometimes the following fact is too hurriedly overlooked: justice does require a judgment because the risk of confusing good and evil could lead an oppressed person to doubt the existence of a good God who rewards the just, besides fostering a sense of impunity on the part of the wicked. Psalm 41 certainly does not say more than this. Broadening this perspective, however, one could say that judgment is necessary even if it goes beyond the human concepts of justice, guilt, punishment, and responsibility. What Psalm 41 is at least saying is that God's judgment is merciful.

Freeing someone from evil is considered an act of the Lord's profound love. The psalmist is delighted by God's presence and experiences a special enjoyment in being able to regain his health. The phrase "raise me up" (v. 10) means making him able to stand up and walk again (both on his own feet and in terms of his faith).

v. 13. Community reading. As we have seen, the unique and unrepeatable experience of the psalmist is received as a legacy of faith by the community and is passed on as a prayer for everyone. The blessing addressed to the Lord and the mention of Israel in this concluding verse confer on the poem a positive and doxological tone. The double repetition of "Amen and amen" has the function of signaling the end of the first book of the Psalter (1-41), but it also serves to add an "exclamation point" to faith in a God who hears the prayer of the needy.

Psalm 42 and Psalm 43

Psalm 42

To the choirmaster.
A Maskil of the Sons of Korah.

¹As a deer longs
　　for flowing streams,
so longs my soul
　　for you, O God.
²My soul thirsts for God,
　　for the living God.
When shall I come and behold
　　the face of God?
³My tears have been my food
　　day and night,
while men say to me continually,
　　"Where is your God?"

⁴These things I remember,
　　as I pour out my soul:
how I went with the throng,
　　and led them in procession to the house of God,
with glad shouts and songs of thanksgiving,
　　a multitude keeping festival.
⁵Why are you cast down, O my soul,
　　and why are you disquieted within me?

Hope in God; for I shall again praise him,
    my savior ⁶and my God.

My soul is cast down within me,
    therefore I remember you
from the land of Jordan and of Hermon,
    from Mount Mizar.
⁷Deep calls to deep
    at the thunder of your cataracts;
all your waves and your billows
    have gone over me.
⁸By day the LORD commands his steadfast love;
    and at night his song is with me,
    a prayer to the God of my life.

⁹I say to God, my rock:
    "Why have you forgotten me?
Why do I go mourning
    because of the oppression of the enemy?"
¹⁰As with a deadly wound in my body,
    my adversaries taunt me,
while they say to me continually,
    "Where is your God?"

¹¹Why are you cast down, O my soul,
    and why are you disquieted within me?
Hope in God; for I shall again praise him,
    my help and my God.

Psalm 43

¹Vindicate me, O God, and defend my cause
    against an ungodly people;
from deceitful and unjust men
    deliver me!

²For you are the God in whom I take refuge;
   why have you cast me off?
Why do I go mourning
   because of the oppression of the enemy?

³Oh, send out your light and your truth;
   let them lead me,
let them bring me to your holy hill
   and to your dwelling!
⁴Then I will go to the altar of God,
   to God my exceeding joy;
and I will praise you with the lyre,
   O God, my God.

⁵Why are you cast down, O my soul,
   and why are you disquieted within me?
Hope in God; for I shall again praise him,
   my savior and my God.

These two poems were originally one psalm. The overall structure of the two together contains a refrain that is repeated three times: "Why are you cast down, O my soul, / and why are you disquieted within me? / Hope in God; for I shall again praise him, / my savior and my God" (Ps 42:5; 42:11; 43:5). This allows us to divide these two interconnected texts into three sections: 42:1-5, the past; 42:6-11, the present; and 43:1-5, the future.

42:1-5. Nostalgia for the past. There is one thought, one image: the deer! The poet projects the state of his own soul onto the animal's anxious search as he himself is restlessly searching for God. This animal is a doe (in Prv 5:19, the wife is described as "a lovely deer, a graceful doe") that represents both fruitfulness (see Gn 49:21) and vibrant young love. (The beloved in the Song of Songs is a "gazelle, or a young stag" [2:9,17; 8:14.]) The soul of the psalmist is panting for God; he is seeking the face of the Lord with his whole *nephesh* (breath, longing, life).

But one question accompanies his urgent impulse: "When shall I come and behold / the face of God?" (v. 2). Being able to contemplate God's face is a desire that runs through many pages of the Old Testament (and the New as well: see 1 Cor 13:12; 2 Cor 4:6). Psalm 27 is nothing but a litany about seeking God's face:

> You have said, "Seek my face."
>> My heart says to you,
> "Your face, LORD, do I seek."
>> Hide not your face from me.
>
> Turn not your servant away in anger,
>> you who have been my help.
> Cast me not off, forsake me not,
>> O God of my salvation! (vv. 8-9)

And yet the man in Psalm 42 is still not ready for this encounter because he knows that only the righteous can have access to God's face ("the upright shall behold his face," Ps 11:7; see also Ps 17:15). The psalmist is aware of the widespread conviction that whoever sees God cannot live (Ex 33:20), even if some privileged people are allowed to have such an encounter (Dt 5:24).

The psalmist finds himself far from God's face. Perhaps he is in exile, so his memories of the times he went to the Temple and participated in joyful processions with liturgical songs make the distance even more bitter (see v. 4). The traditional phrase "come see the face of God" describes the solemn entry of the people into the Temple (Ps 95:6; 105:2-4; Ps 122:1). In verse 4 the psalmist says, "I pour out my soul." The verb *shaphak* here means, "dissolve, pour out, cast down," and it describes the psalmist's inner state as he is feeling himself "poured out" like liquid. When he says, "My tears have been my food day and night" (v. 3), he is using a metaphor for deep, prolonged sorrow ("You have fed them with the bread of tears, / and given them tears to drink in full measure,"

Ps 80:5; "For I eat ashes like bread, / and mingle tears with my drink," Ps 102:9).

In his state of debility, the man is being asked a theological question: "Where is your God?" (v. 3). This blasphemous and sarcastic cry is probably leveled by the oppressors (the Babylonians) who interpret the defeat of Israel and its exile — in line with religious conceptions of the ancient Near East — as a form of weakness on the part of their divinity. The question makes the man's condition even more painful, and it recurs in other passages in the Bible: "Why should the nations say, 'Where is their God?'" (Ps 79:10; Ps 115:2; see also Jl 2:17; Mi 7:10).

The most representative silence of God in the Bible is certainly in the Book of Job, a muteness that can cause someone to doubt God's goodness:

> "I cry to you and you do not answer me;
>> I stand, and you do not heed me.
> You have turned cruel to me;
>> with the might of your hand you persecute me.
> You lift me up on the wind, you make me ride on it,
>> and you toss me about in the roar of the storm.
> Yes, I know that you will bring me to death,
>> and to the house appointed for all living." (30:20-23)

At the height of his breaking point he ends up sighing, "Oh, that I had one to hear me! / (Here is my signature! let the Almighty answer me!)" (Jb 31:35). God's silence is more excruciating for Job than the wounds in his leprous body.

In verse 5 the refrain that serves as an antiphon appears for the first time. The psalmist, almost as if he is split in two, addresses his soul from two different vantage points. The first is expressed in his question, "Why are you cast down, O my soul, / and why are you disquieted within me?" His sadness is described by a verb that indicates a state of crushing despondency (see Ps 44:25) or discouragement — as if he were in a deep, dark pit (Ps 57:6). His second address to himself implies a request for rehabilitation that will be heard, a restoration of his position in the sight of God and the defeat of the men who deride him: "Hope in God; for I shall again praise him" (v. 5; see also Is 63:9). Proof of his reinstatement would be the possibility of continuing to praise God, of being able to make a public profession of faith without fear of being mocked and derided.

42:6-11. The bitter present. The psalmist leads us through his "inner geography" (the Jordan River, the highest mountain of the Promised Land, Hermon, and Mount Mizar). The sadness of his present condition of exile makes the memory of the past even more bitter. In the first stanza God is presented as "water" that can quench thirst, but in this second section, water, still referring to God, has a more negative connotation. It is, in fact, God's devastating power that has taken the psalmist far away from the Promised Land. Water is therefore presented in an ambivalent manner. Great waters and rivers have either a mythic connotation in describing the supremacy of YHWH over chaos or primordial waters (see Ps 74:14-15; 77:17-19; 107:24-25,29; Is 43:2) or a historical significance in reference to the enemies of Israel that God defeats (Ps 144:7; Is 17:12-13; Jer 46:6-8; Ezek 32:2,13-14). Only YHWH can rescue someone from the deadly waters of the abyss and from *sheol*, the underworld, as we also see in Jonah 2:2-6. As the metaphor indicates, it is God who caused the exile ("all your waves and your billows / have gone over me," v. 7), and that is due historically to God's punishment of Israel for its sin, first and foremost, idolatry.

But now, in the midst of so much dejection and torment, divine mercy (*hesed*) appears as a daily gift offered by the Lord to his faithful: "By day the Lord commands his steadfast love" (v. 8). It is only thanks to this loving attitude on God's part that even the night, which follows the day, but also the night of faith, can be filled with song and prayer. In verse 5 the praying man identified the proof of his rescue as being able to praise God again. Moses refers to the divine name "the God of the spirits of all flesh" in Numbers 27:16 as he guides his people; analogously we can apply the meaning of this divine name to the psalmist, who longs to resume walking on his own path and his community's path.

"God, my rock," in verse 9, creates a strong contrast with God-as-water. This phrase, generally used only in war contexts, recalls the firm strength of the Lord, his power to defeat his enemies (see 2 Sm 22:2; Ps 18:2; 31:3; 62:2,6; 92:15; 144:1). Although "rock" translates the word *sela'* in this psalm, in other contexts the same concept is found in words with the root *'mn*, which evokes the concept of constancy and stability (1 Sm 2:35; 2 Sm 7:16; 2 Chr 20:20; Is 7:9). Connected to this concept is trustworthiness (Dt 7:9; Is 49:7) and truthfulness (Gn 42:20; Ps 19:7; 93:5), whose direct reference point and main source is God (Gn 24:27; 2 Sm 2:6; Ps 71:22; 88:11; 89:1-2,5).

The questions in verse 9 — "Why have you forgotten me? / Why do I go mourning / because of the oppression of the enemy?" — are typical questions in a lamentation, and wait for an answer from God. In fact, the psalmist attributes to him the responsibility for his condition, which he likens to butchery by the enemy. In verse 10 the Hebrew for the "deadly wound" here is "broken bones," an image also found in Psalm 51:8 that refers to the inner physical structure of the man shattered by the piercing theological question, "Where is your God?" It is another way of describing the terrible situation of psychological suffering in which he finds himself. The second section of the poem ends with verse 11 reiterating the refrain full of hope in verse 5.

43:1-5. The bright future. With typical legal language, the psalmist asks God for justice because he feels falsely accused (see Ps 7:8; 26:1; 35:23-24). The picture of the wicked is sketched out with the most common profile in the Bible for criminals. They are ruthless, literally "without mercy (*hesed*)," and clearly lack the virtue that is a hallmark of God's character. The adjective "deceitful" conveys the idea of someone who fosters an attitude of lies (Ps 24:4) and of deceit (like Jacob who robbed Esau of his birthright in Genesis 27:35).

Verse 2 substantially repeats verse 9 in Psalm 42. It performs the function of emphasizing God's fundamental role in resolving the conflict between this man and his enemies. The man hopes for specific methods of divine intervention (see v. 3): God's light and truth. As if light and truth were God's two wings, so to speak, he would like to be carried away from Babylon and lifted up to the mountain of God, which we can identify as Mount Zion, the place in which God dwells (Is 11:9; 66:20). It is an idealization of Jerusalem (Ps 3:4; 15:1; 48:1-2; 99:9; 147:2,12) and refers overall to the Promised Land.

The altar of God in verse 4 is the ultimate goal of the journey. The psalm opens with the nostalgic memory of processions to the Temple, and now it ends with the same liturgical image. So what has changed in the psalmist's soul by the end of the poem? If nostalgia and discouragement dominate on the memory level, at another, more profound level the awareness of an assured salvific intervention has now made inroads. This is in line with the theme of increasing trust in the second book of the Psalter. It makes the condition of exile less bitter because the Lord dwells in the psalmist's heart and is already making him sense his presence, a presence in the midst of absence.

Psalm 51

To the choirmaster. A Psalm of David,
when Nathan the prophet came to him,
after he had gone in to Bathsheba.

[1]Have mercy on me, O God,
> according to your merciful love;
> according to your abundant mercy blot out my
> transgressions.

[2]Wash me thoroughly from my iniquity,
> and cleanse me from my sin!

[3]For I know my transgressions,
> and my sin is ever before me.

[4]Against you, you only, have I sinned,
> and done that which is evil in your sight,
so that you are justified in your sentence
> and blameless in your judgment.

[5]Behold, I was brought forth in iniquity,
> and in sin did my mother conceive me.

[6]Behold, you desire truth in the inward being;
> therefore teach me wisdom in my secret heart.

[7]Purge me with hyssop, and I shall be clean;
> wash me, and I shall be whiter than snow.

[8]Make me hear joy and gladness;
>   let the bones which you have broken rejoice.
[9]Hide your face from my sins,
>   and blot out all my iniquities.

[10]Create in me a clean heart, O God,
>   and put a new and right spirit within me.
[11]Cast me not away from your presence,
>   and take not your holy Spirit from me.
[12]Restore to me the joy of your salvation,
>   and uphold me with a willing spirit.

[13]Then I will teach transgressors your ways,
>   and sinners will return to you.
[14]Deliver me from bloodguilt, O God,
>   O God of my salvation,
>   and my tongue will sing aloud of your deliverance.

[15]O Lord, open my lips,
>   and my mouth shall show forth your praise.
[16]For you take no delight in sacrifice;
>   were I to give a burnt offering, you would not be pleased.
[17]The sacrifice acceptable to God is a broken spirit;
>   a broken and contrite heart, O God, you will not despise.

[18]Do good to Zion in your good pleasure;
>   rebuild the walls of Jerusalem,
[19]then will you delight in right sacrifices,
>   in burnt offerings and whole burnt offerings;
>   then bulls will be offered on your altar.

The title and v. 1. The sin with Bathsheba. The heading refers to King David's acknowledgement of his sexual sin as recounted in 2 Samuel 12:1-14. David has committed adultery with Uriah's wife, and when the prophet Nathan denounces him, he requests forgiveness for his great sin. The liturgical tradition has always interpreted Psalm 51 in this vein and considered it one of the seven penitential psalms (along with Psalms 6, 32, 38, 102, 130, 143). It is called *Miserere* ("Have mercy") for good reason.

vv. 1-9. Confession of guilt and request for forgiveness of sin. This represents the heart of the poem because it describes the condition of the penitent's soul as he admits his transgression and invokes divine mercy.

vv. 1-2. Request for purification. Three different words are used for "sin." It is important to note that these three words are often placed next to one another to express the totality of a transgression. In Leviticus 16, which describes the liturgy for the great atonement called *Yom Kippur*, for example, the sanctuary is defiled because of Israel's sins (*hatta'im*), transgressions (*pesha'im*), and iniquity (*'aon*). We already explained the first two words (*hatta't* and *pesha'*) in reading other psalms.

Hatta't, because of its generic nature, is the word most frequently used in the Old Testament (595 times). As earlier indicated in the commentary on Psalm 25, it refers to the idea of failing to attain a moral or religious goal. The sinner is someone who does not follow the right trajectory and is moving away from the target (see Jgs 20:16).

The word *pesha'* recalls a wide range of meanings and seems to relate to a rupture of legal harmony with a person (God or a neighbor) or with the community. That harmony needs to be restored through a process, unless someone who has valid legal rights abandons legal action and concedes forgiveness.

The prophetic tradition speaks against political wrongdoing, the oppression of the poor, idolatry, and defiling the Temple (see Am 1-2). The word *pesha'* occurs in 1 Kings 8:50 when Solomon lifts up a prayer to YHWH at the altar before the people. In his public request for forgiveness it is clear that the sins of Israel for which pardon is being sought are transgressions against YHWH. A similar use of *pesha'* can also be found in the Book of Jeremiah, where the sin of the people of Israel is that of abandoning their relationship with God and devoting themselves to idolatry and adultery (5:6-8). The word refers to the social and religious rebellion that sully people and for which purification is necessary.

The third word linked to sin is *'aon* and is used for sins against God (see Ex 20:5; Dt 5:9; Is 1:4; Jer 11:10), but also for sins against other people. These kinds of sins against other people are linked chiefly to infractions in ritual practices due to sexual behavior (2 Sm 3:8). In Ezekiel 18:30, for example, the invitation to conversion is aimed at freeing Israel from a rebellion that is a real stumbling block of iniquity (*mikshol 'aon*), rebellion that in the preceding verses is described as conduct that people need to avoid. The wicked person is described there as someone "who ... eats upon the mountains, defiles his neighbor's wife, oppresses the poor and needy, commits robbery, does not restore the pledge, lifts up his eyes to the idols, commits abomination, lends at interest, and takes increase; shall he then live? He shall not live. He has done all these abominable things; he shall surely die; his blood shall be upon himself" (Ez 18:11-13).

This psalm requests these three sins to be, respectively, blotted out (*mahah*), washed (*kabas*), and cleansed (*taher*). The first verb is linked to the legal and commercial world (see Ex 32:32-33; Nm 5:23) and means "to cancel" a contract or written document (Ex 17:14; Dt 9:14). Sin is paralleled to a contracted debt that has legal written proof. The ordinary context of *kabas* concerns laundry: people wash away their sins as though they are washing clothes and objects. This approach arose in the priestly tradition in which practices for ritual purity and holiness allowed people to draw near to the sphere of the holy (Ex 19:10,14; Lv 6:25-27; 11:25,28,40). The third verb (*taher*), close to the Arabic and Aramaic root *zhr*, "to shine," evokes the idea of splendor. Sin darkens things or makes them opaque; the person or the situation has lost its luminosity and needs to be brought back to its natural splendor (for example, after childbirth, Lv 12:7; leprosy, Lv 13; 14; 22:4; sexual discharge, Lv 15; 22:4; Dt 23:10-11; contact with dead bodies, Lv 21:1-4; Nm 6:6-

9). The psalmist invokes, however, God's full divine pardon for the complete range of his sins and makes appeal to the merciful love of God, to his *hesed*, his loving faithfulness. *Hanan*, in verse 1, means "to have mercy, to have pity, to be gracious to someone."

vv. 3-6. Confession of sin. After he asks for forgiveness, the penitent's first act is to admit his sin again. Taking stock of his situation without hiding it expresses the attitude of someone who is open to reconciliation with God (see Ps 32:5; 38:18). On the other hand, people who hide their guilt not only do not have psychological awareness of themselves, but also have only a partial understanding of God because they perceive him with fear. In verse 3, not only does he not hide his sin, he also says directly that his *pesha'* is almost obsessively present in his mind. The sin committed against people (according to the psalm's header, adultery) is in the end a sin against God (v. 4). This is why, after Uriah's murder and adultery with his wife, David says, "I have sinned against the LORD" (2 Sm 12:13). The justice of God is blameless; the sinful action has injured the innocent party in the relationship, so the psalmist now asks pardon, knowing full well that the offended party could punish the offense by issuing a sentence of condemnation (Ez 28:2; Sir 36:7-10).

In verse 5 the psalmist repeats a profession of his state of sin: he has been radically immersed in the reality of sin from his conception. That conviction is rooted in the Bible's declaration of the tragic human condition beginning with the account in Genesis 3: people are unable to appear before God because they are essentially unrighteous (see Ps 143:2), because since their youth their hearts have inclined toward evil (Gn 8:21). The rarely used verb *yhm* expresses the state of animals in heat (Gn 30:38,41). One could think that such an instinct would be linked to the moment of copulation as a sinful act in itself that wounds the beginning of any new life. In the history of interpretation, in fact, verse 5 has been interpreted as proof of the impurity of the sexual union even in marriage. To all appearances, however, the text does not intend to say that, but intensifies the perspective of the penitent who senses his long-standing natural propensity to sin.

The sincerity (*'emet*) manifested by the penitent is a basis upon which a reversal can occur: it is true that the inclination to evil dwells in the human heart, but it is also true that God can give wisdom that directs someone toward a new existence (see v. 6). The teaching of wisdom does not involve a merely passive substitution (a simple "heart transplant") but a dynamic aspect because the teaching is linked to life and permeates its many phases. God is presented as an expert teacher who educates a disciple disposed to receive training, as we read in Isaiah 54:13: "All your sons shall be taught by the LORD, / and great shall be the prosperity of your sons."

vv. 7-9. Invocation for purification. There is a direct correlation between these verses and verses 1-3, because the same verbs are used. Hyssop is related to oregano, an aromatic plant known for its sterilizing properties. It is sprinkled in the homes of lepers (see Lv 14:4,6) and during sacrifices for the expiation of sin (Nm 19:6,18). The concept of sprinkling is also found in reference to the blood of the covenant at Sinai (Ex 24:8). The value of hyssop and its propitiatory function of being sprinkled recalls the ritual of the paschal lamb in which the lintels of the doorposts are sprinkled with blood (Ex 12:22). The other element that points to catharsis is snow, which is more directly referred to in Isaiah: "Come now, let us reason together, / says the LORD: / though your sins are like scarlet, / they shall be as white as snow; / though they are red like crimson, / they shall become like wool" (Is 1:18). Verse 7 makes clear that the darkness or filthiness of sin is purged and he becomes white as snow. (Snow is rarely seen in Israel, so it is more beautiful for people there; see Sir 43:18).

The traditional link of sin-punishment explains the state of well-being described in verse 8: if sin causes even physical affliction, it is logical that when it is pardoned people would experience joy and health for their whole being. Bones indicate the innermost part of a person's physical structure (see Jb 7:15), so they participate in the full vigor of life that comes forth again. The verb "to hear" is used to express the psalmist's perception of the new state of his soul. This is analogous to what we read in Isaiah 66:14: "You shall see, and your heart shall rejoice; / your bones shall flourish like the grass; / and it shall be known that the hand of the LORD is with his servants, / and his indignation is against his enemies."

If sin can reduce a person to being like a skeleton, forgiveness restores his flesh (see Ez 37). Therefore, the request for mercy that permeates this first part of the psalm is repeated, and he asks God, after having admitted his failings, not to look at them any more (v. 9).

vv. 10-19. A request for a new relationship with God. After acknowledging the full range of his own transgressions and the root of his sinfulness, the psalmist requests a new relationship with God that will no longer be marked by weakness but by the strength that derives from the penitent's new condition.

Verses 10-12 focus on the heart and spirit. The first imperative verb, "create," marks the turning point in the psalm. The verb "create" (*bara'*) applies only to God (see Gn 1:1) because he is the only one who can bring things into being from nothing (Ps 104:30; 148:5). The re-creation of the man involves the heart (*lev*), which is the center of mind and will, but also the breath of life (*ruah*) (Gn 2:7). The heart and spirit recall the new covenant in Jeremiah 31:33 in which God himself will establish a new covenant not on tablets of stone but in the innermost recesses of the human heart. Along with a clean heart the psalmist asks for a right spirit (*nakon*) — that is, a firm, strong, steadfast spirit no longer at the mercy of an inclination to evil — a spirit with "backbone," so to speak. There is another characterization of this new spirit in verse 12: a "willing spirit" that is open and obedient. The imperative verbs "restore" and "uphold" express the idea that the qualities of this new spirit — the new architecture or structure supporting the penitent — are developed as he walks the path that leads to full renewal. Like the teaching of wisdom in verse 6, this, too, is the beginning of his new condition.

Verse 11 mentions another spirit, God's spirit. It is defined as "holy" (*qadosh*) because only God is the absolute Holy One (see Is 6:3), whereas human beings become holy only by conforming their lives to God's holiness and separating themselves from uncleanness and impurity (Ex 19:6; Is 62:12; 63:18; Jer 2:3). Not being admitted into God's presence is the equivalent of being rejected by him, not listened to by him, and thus not reintegrated into his loving plan. When YHWH withdraws, a break in the relationship of trust is thereby decreed (as with Saul in 1 Sm 28) and a break in the covenant is decreed (as in the reign of Israel and Judah in 2 Kings 17:20; 24:20). The presence (or the face) of God and his holy spirit are, then, images of the same divine person who actively turns to the penitent in a benevolent manner.

In verses 13-17 the psalmist makes a commitment. As often happens in supplications, the man proposes to take on a task that will demonstrate his intentions: gratitude for his deliverance will be transformed into a missionary and catechetical song as the sinner becomes a preacher. His drama becomes an example, and the wisdom he acquires after forgiveness will be communicated as an effective instrument to combat the folly of sin. Praise of God is the best offering he can give (see v. 15); it is worth more than burnt offerings and ritual sacrifices. Everything is made new in the life of the one who has experienced forgiveness: heart, spirit, bones, mouth, lips, tongue.

The phrase in verse 14, "deliver me from bloodguilt," can be explained by its connection to Uriah's homicide by David (see 2 Sm 12:9-10), or it could also refer to an unspecified sin of shedding blood (Jer 26:15). It is, though, his last request for definitive deliverance from the serious sin that has stained him.

In verses 16-17 the psalmist formulates his intention not to stop at the external level of worship. The main thrust expressed here, and in all of Psalm 50 to which this psalm is closely tied, is that the true sacrifice is a person's heart (see Is 1:11-13,16-17; Jer 6:20; Hos 6:6; Am 5:21-24).

vv. 18-19. Community ending. The last two verses are an addition that comes from the time of exile or the beginning of the postexilic period. As often happens in the Psalms, the community feels the need to actualize the content of the poem, reading it in the light of the events that mark their history. The deportation to Babylon becomes a punishment for sin, and once the community is purged it can again address a prayer to the Lord for the rebuilding of the holy city (see Neh 2:17-20) and for rebuilding the Temple for sacrifice (Is 62:6-7). The "sacrifice" mentioned in verse 19 is a burnt offering (*'olah*). Sacrifice usually refers to the slitting of an animal's throat (Gn 31:54; 46:1), but here it is compared to a burnt offering (Ex 10:25) because the slaughtered animal is often partially burnt. A burnt offering burns the whole or part of the animal (Lv 16:25,27), and it occurs on the Temple altar that usually has a fire burning (Lv 6:9). This expresses the aspect of the gift of sacrifice that is offered as recounted in Leviticus 9:12-14, in which the burnt offering is offered first, followed by the sin offering for the people. The community rereading of the psalm reaches the conclusion that if, during the exile, sacrifice was represented by bitter weeping (Ps 137:1), it is now time for a more appropriate and proper liturgy that is well pleasing to God, since it is inspired by a humbled heart.

Psalm 57

To the choirmaster: according to Do Not Destroy.
A Miktam of David, when he fled
from Saul, in the cave.

¹Be merciful to me, O God, be merciful to me,
 for in you my soul takes refuge;
in the shadow of your wings I will take refuge,
 till the storms of destruction pass by.
²I cry to God Most High,
 to God who fulfils his purpose for me.
³He will send from heaven and save me,
 he will put to shame those who trample upon me.
       [Selah]
God will send forth his mercy and his faithfulness!

⁴I lie in the midst of lions
 that greedily devour the sons of men;
their teeth are spears and arrows,
 their tongues sharp swords.

⁵Be exalted, O God, above the heavens!
 Let your glory be over all the earth!

⁶They set a net for my steps;
 my soul was bowed down.

They dug a pit in my way,
  but they have fallen into it themselves. [Selah]

⁷My heart is steadfast, O God,
  my heart is steadfast!
I will sing and make melody!
  ⁸Awake, my soul!
Awake, O harp and lyre!
  I will awake the dawn!
⁹I will give thanks to you, O Lord, among the peoples;
  I will sing praises to you among the nations.
¹⁰For your mercy is great to the heavens,
  your faithfulness to the clouds.

¹¹ Be exalted, O God, above the heavens!
  Let your glory be over all the earth!

This psalm is presented as a supplication addressed to God. The entire heading, "To the choirmaster . . ." appears with minor variations in Psalms 57, 58, and 59, so it is a clear signal that the editor believed they should be read together.

The First Book of Samuel, Chapter 24, tells the story of the encounter between David and King Saul, his father-in-law, who has gone out with his army to kill David. The Lord gives David, who was already anointed by Samuel but not yet ruling, an advantage over Saul in the desert of Engedi. The cave mentioned in the heading is in the area of the Wildgoats' Rocks (see 1 Sm 24:3), where David could have easily gotten the upper hand over his father-in-law since the Lord had put Saul and his men to sleep. Approaching Saul in the cave, David only cuts off the skirt of his robe instead of killing him. David follows Saul after he leaves the cave and shows him the piece he has cut off. Saul realizes David could have killed him, and David asks him to stop persecuting him. Saul had wanted to kill David due to envy because he feared losing the kingdom, but he ceases his hostility and no longer pursues David.

Psalm 57 is ascribed to David and bears witness to feelings of both anxiety and trust at this juncture. The structure of the poem is very simple and indicates its two separate parts by ending each with the repetition of the refrain, "Be exalted, O God, above the heavens! / Let your glory be over all the earth!"

vv. 1-5. Supplication. The opening of the psalm is typical of supplications (see Ps 51:1-2; 56:1). The verb *hanan* ("be merciful") is repeated twice, followed by a profession of faith in God-our-refuge. (This is, of course, applicable to David actually seeking refuge in a cave.)

In verse 1, "my soul" (*nephesh* in Hebrew) refers to the whole man who seeks refuge under the Lord's wings until the danger can be warded off. The beautiful image of wings is typical in Deuteronomy. We will see it again later in the commentary on Psalm 103, and it is borrowed from Deuteronomy 32:11, where the wings of the eagle lift up the people of Israel. This is the first use of an animal symbol in the poem, and it evokes the strength and ardent protection of the Lord. God is called "God Most High" (v. 2), continuing the image of the great bird that glides on high. If any danger comes from below (enemies, and in this case Saul), the Lord carries people high up and far from the snares of men.

In verse 3, the two wings under which the man who is praying finds shelter are mercy and faithfulness, qualities that express the intimate nature of God's involvement in humanity's history. When God reveals himself he does so by manifesting a power inspired by love. The reference to the event of the Exodus, because of the combination of "mercy and faithfulness," found in Exodus 34:6, is very appropriate because freedom from slavery is described in terms of being lifted up on the wings of the Lord: "You have seen what I did to the Egyptians, and how I bore you on eagles' wings and brought you to myself" (Ex 19:4). The whole texture of Psalm 57 is woven together by paraphrasing the history of salvation and applying it to the experience of the man who is undergoing harsh oppression by his enraged enemies.

The second image drawn from the animal kingdom is that of the lion in verse 4. Lions are described in terms of war language: their teeth are like spears and arrows while their words are like sharp swords. These images are traditional representations often seen in the Psalter (see Ps 7:2; 10:9; 11:2; 37:14; 52:1,4; 58:6). The image becomes even more vivid with the psalmist's mention of lying down. He even has to share a bed with his enemies, perhaps wanting to indicate that his worst enemies are living in the same space, the same house. The link between Saul and David, father-in-law and son-in-law, clarifies this statement, but the idea that the worst conflicts can arise within families should not be dismissed. (See, for example, Jacob and Esau, Joseph and his brothers, in Genesis 27-50.)

One other reference that can broaden out the psalm's meaning concerns Daniel in the lions' den. His predicament is a sign of the safety the Lord gives to his faithful. Daniel tames the lions and spends the whole night with them (see Dn 6:19-24). In the Hebrew version, lions are described in Psalm 57:4 as "inflamed by rage." This hyperbolical expression could connect to another passage in the Book of Daniel in which we read that Shadrach, Meshach, and Abednego, three Jewish youths who refuse to worship the statue of the king, are thrown into the fiery furnace by the king of Babylon but come out unscathed (Dn 3).

The refrain in verse 5 ends the first section. Having recourse to the cosmic-spatial symbolism of heaven and earth, the psalmist speaks about God's power extending above the heavens, meaning, it is unlimited. Even heaven, generally considered the place in which God dwells, cannot contain him (see 1 Kgs 8:27; 2 Chr 2:6). At this point in the poem, verse 5 becomes an invocation by the man who finds himself in difficulty; he hopes God can display his "heaviness." The word "glory" (*kabod*) actually means "weight," and by extension can signify "importance" or "relevance." The expression appears to be a synthesis of Psalm 8:1 ("how majestic is your name in all the earth") and Isaiah 6:3 ("the whole earth is full of his glory"). In these texts it is primarily God who is at the center of the scene (in creation and in the Temple, respectively), but so is the man who feels connected to this presence that is changing his life.

vv. 6-11. Thanksgiving. The second section weaves together the image of a net and images of joy and singing typical of a hymn that is an invitation to praise, and it ends with the refrain in verse 11 that serves as the final antiphon.

The law of counterpoint is admirably set forth in verse 6. In the Bible, there is a kind of balance willed by God according to which evil backfires sooner or later on its author, on the basis of a retribution that is innate to the works themselves: "These men lie in wait for their own blood, / they set an ambush for their own lives. / Such are the ways of all who get gain by violence; / it takes away the life of its possessors" (Prv 1:18-19). The author of Sirach formulates this law in a clear way: "He who digs a pit will fall into it, / and he who sets a snare will be caught in it. / If a man does evil, it will roll back upon him, / and he will not know where it came from" (Sir 27:26-27). The reflection of Bildad, one of Job's three friends, is along this line, concerning the lot of the wicked man who is caught in his own net and falls into his own trap (see Jb 18:7-10).

The psalmist asks for justice and wants to be taken out of the clutches of his enemies. In verse 6, he indirectly professes his trust in divine workings because he knows that whoever does evil will become the victim of his own wicked perpetrations in the end. This also explains the phrase in verse 3 that God "will put to shame those who trample on me." The man, renouncing both his desire for vengeance and trying to achieve justice on his own, entrusts himself to God, who will foil the plots of his enemies and confound them.

He uses the word "heart" (*lev*) twice in verse 7. It needs to be noted that the heart is the center of a person, because in the majority of cases intellectual and rational functions are attributed to the heart. That is the case in 1 Kings 3:9-12 when Solomon asks God for an "understanding mind" (*lev*) — that is, the necessary wisdom and discernment to govern the people. Heart also indicates the central organ that controls the motor abilities of the body's different members (see 1 Sm 25:37-39). But above all it refers to what is hidden and is not immediately evident, the most intimate part of human beings, their temperaments, as in 1 Samuel 16:7. Samuel is in Bethlehem to anoint David as king of Israel, and the criterion to recognize the future king is not his physical appearance but the young boy's generosity of heart, which only God can know. The heart, according to most modern perspectives, is also the place of feelings, the emotive sphere of sentiments. It is modulated by the situation in which people find themselves and covers the entire gamut of human emotions, from the deepest anguish to the most radiant joy (Ps 25:16-17). As is the case for the soul (*nephesh*), so, too, the heart has an innate connection to acts of desiring and longing (Ps 21:2; Prv 6:25).

In Psalm 57, the strength the man feels is highlighted together with his resolute will to express his current joyful state. A heart that is steadfast (*nakon*), an adjective also used in Psalm 51:12, declares the penitent's new reality. In this psalm the man presents his new condition almost as a rebirth, alluded to in his reference to "the dawn" of a new day. The logic of the psalm seems to indicate a bifurcation in the man who no longer speaks to God but is speaking to himself and does not know how to express his joy; one could almost say he "is jumping out of his skin" for joy.

After addressing himself and his musical instruments, the man begins his song in verses 9-10. We can distinguish a dual movement in his praise: a vertical movement that reaches up to heaven at its furthest unreachable point, and a horizontal movement toward all the people who dwell on earth. God's mercy, in other words, fills the universe and reaches all the people on earth. The man who is praying seizes on this dynamic and feels himself fully involved in it. Like an oil stain, so to speak, divine love spreads out from the center of this man's heart to the most inaccessible places.

The refrain in verse 11 closes out the second section, as well as the whole psalm, and functions to put a seal on the mystical summits he has reached. The psalmist does not tell us if he has been freed from his enemies or not, but he ends on a note of divine mercy, almost forgetting his own suffering. In other words, it does not matter if the enemies' threats are still raging, because what counts is the boundless love of the Lord, which is the best security a faithful person can have in the midst of difficulty.

Psalm 92

A Song for the Sabbath.

¹It is good to give thanks to the LORD,
    to sing praises to your name, O Most High;
²to declare your merciful love in the morning,
    and your faithfulness by night,
³to the music of the lute and the harp,
    to the melody of the lyre.
⁴For you, O LORD, have made me glad by your work;
    at the works of your hands I sing for joy.

⁵How great are your works, O LORD!
    Your thoughts are very deep!
⁶The dull man cannot know,
    the stupid cannot understand this:
⁷that, though the wicked sprout like grass
    and all evildoers flourish,
they are doomed to destruction for ever,
    ⁸but you, O LORD, are on high for ever.
⁹For, behold, your enemies, O LORD,
    for, behold, your enemies shall perish;
    all evildoers shall be scattered.

¹⁰But you have exalted my horn like that of the wild ox;
    You have poured over me fresh oil.

[11]My eyes have seen the downfall of my enemies,
    my ears have heard the doom of my evil assailants.

[12]The righteous flourish like the palm tree,
    and grow like a cedar in Lebanon.
[13]They are planted in the house of the LORD,
    they flourish in the courts of our God.
[14]They still bring forth fruit in old age,
    they are ever full of sap and green,
[15]to show that the LORD is upright;
    he is my rock, and there is no unrighteousness in him.

This psalm is a typical example of a hymn and can be subdivided into three sections. First, there is an invitation to praise with stringed instruments (vv. 1-3). Next, the body of the hymn presents the reasons for that praise, which is the recompense of the just (vv. 4-13). The conclusion is a renewed invitation to acknowledge the righteousness of God (vv. 14-15). The inspiration for the psalm could have been an instruction by a teacher presented in this form of a prayer-song. The heading links the psalm to the celebration of the Sabbath day.

vv. 1–3. Invitation to praise the Lord (YHWH). The first verse uses the adjective "good" (*tov*), which appears in the Old Testament 741 times. It has three primary meanings. The first is ethical — for example, in relation to the goodness of YHWH as in Psalm 34:8. In this sense, good is the opposite of "evil" (see Am 5:14). The second meaning is functional and concerns the suitability or appropriateness of one thing as opposed to another (Ex 14:12; Nm 14:3; 1 Sm 27:1). Its third meaning is aesthetic and refers to the beauty of the human body and people's fascination with it (Gn 6:2; 24:16; 26:7; 2 Sm 11:2; Est 2:2,3,7). Psalm 92 is the only psalm that begins with this adjective in the Hebrew, and it recalls the use of the introductory phrase "Blessed is ... " that begins other psalms (Ps 1:1; 32:1-2; 41:1; 112:1).

The goodness of giving thanks to God in the song never ceases. Thanksgiving goes on from morning to evening and all through the night. God's merciful love (*hesed*) and faithfulness (*'emunah*) in verse 2 are the divine attributes being praised. These words characterize God's action to such an extent that they become personified in Psalm 85:10 and Psalm 89:14.

It is difficult to know which instruments are referred to, especially since the Hebrew word for the number "ten" is used to describe the first instrument, merely indicating an instrument with many strings that sounds like a harp or something similar. The Psalter uses such instruments to describe the very spirit of praise in which the lyrics and the music harmonize to express the joy of the man who is praying.

vv. 4–13. The body of the hymn. The repetition of the conjunction "For" at the beginning of verses 4 and 9 signals the two main sections of this praise text (vv. 4-8 and 9-13).

The Lord is stronger than the wicked. Verses 4 and 5 focus on YHWH. He is the reason for the psalmist's joy, because of his marvels and "the works of your hands," a phrase that is a fixed expression for his action as Creator (see Ps 8:6; 143:5). The sequence of God's "works" and "thoughts" in these verses focuses on the visibility of God's intervention the man is experiencing. God's love is a solid fact, so this is not just a vague, gratuitous proclamation on the man's part. Insistence on this theological fact seems to have a very clear basis because verses 6-7 point to an anomaly on a higher plane glimpsed by the psalmist: his experiences are, in fact, not universal in the sense that they are not shared by all his fellow human beings. For example, the *dull* man cannot know these things and the *stupid* man cannot understand them. The first man and especially the second man belong to the category of individuals who lack necessary understanding, so they need instruction (Prv 5:13; 15:32; 18:2). The linking together of these individuals emphasizes a moral dimension: the dull man is the violent man, while the stupid man is someone who provokes others imprudently and begins arguments. Not only do they not understand, but being stubborn they also do not want to understand.

Verse 7 explicitly mentions the wicked and the evildoers in general who cannot know and appreciate God's marvelous works. According to the Book of Wisdom, they tempt God and put him to the test, talking nonsense about him, and they do not have righteous intentions. For that reason they are excluded from his presence and from knowing his plans (see 1:2-4). Judgment about them is clear: just as the grass appears for a moment, so the flourishing of evildoers is only a temporary phenomenon. In addition, the brevity of their lives on earth is followed by eternal ruin.

Psalm 92 shares the theme of just retribution with Psalms 37 and 73 in which the flourishing of the evildoers is a problem, because, according to the traditional theory of just rewards, they should succumb to and suffer sickness, misery, and death. In Psalm 92, this issue, which risks getting complicated, as it does for Job and Qoheleth, is resolved by a confession of faith: "You ... are on high for ever" (v. 8). YHWH's superiority means there is no risk of any temporary hindering of his plans, because he rules over everything from his position on high. "He is on high" is a phrase that has historical and mythical connotations: he is higher than all the other gods, and he is inaccessible and invincible (see Jb 31:2; Mi 6:6). Isaiah 57:15 fully expresses the sense of verse 8:

> For thus says the high and lofty One
>   who inhabits eternity, whose name is Holy:
> "I dwell in the high and holy place,
>   and also with him who is of a contrite and humble spirit,
> to revive the spirit of the humble,
>   and to revive the heart of the contrite."

vv. 9-13. The flourishing strength of the righteous. After the declaration in verse 8 that the Lord is on high, verse 9 reaffirms the clear conviction that evildoers will be punished. They are called "enemies" twice in this verse to confirm the negative profile that has been drawn of them up to now. Like grass, their lives are doomed, and they will perish and be scattered.

The image of the wild ox in verse 10 is particularly suggestive. The psalmist, who has regained his conviction of faith in the face of potential humiliation by evildoers, is presented as a wild ox full of muscular strength, an untamable animal who does not submit to being used in farming (see Jb 39:9-12). The ox's rage lets him get the upper hand over his enemies (Nm 23:22; 24:8; Dt 33:17; Ps 22:21; Is 34:7). We can say that the symbol of the wild ox commonly conveys the concept of fierce strength and power. In the ancient Near East a lunar bull came to be adored as a sacred animal or deity, associated with the Great Mother (*Magna Mater*) and later with the god Mithras. Large bovine were painted on Ishtar's gate in Babylon, and the animals' horns were meant to ward off evil. It is not by accident that the Hebrew word the psalm uses for "strength" is *qeren*, meaning "horn" (Ps 75:4-5; 89:17). In the Egyptian language, the symbol of the horn (as well as the arm and the foreleg) indicates "strength."

The anointing in verse 10 ("You have poured over me fresh oil") tones the muscles, makes them gleam, and prepares them for battle. The man who is praying moves from a description of strength in nature to the very human context of the challenge from his enemies in verse 11; looking straight at them expresses his courage and scornful disdain. A dual reference to oil and seeing occurs in Psalm 23:5 as well, where the man in that psalm can peacefully sit at table, secure under the gaze of his adversaries who have now been rendered harmless. To "have heard the doom" of his enemies in verse 11 means to be aware of the adversity that has befallen them and of the reestablishment of the justice that was announced in the preceding verses, even though the manner of the reversal for his situation is not specified.

The second symbol that dominates Psalm 92 is the palm tree in verses 12 and 13. This image opens the Psalter in Psalm 1:3 where the righteous person is compared to a tree that always bears fruit and never withers. In Psalm 92 the emphasis is not so much on fruit as on the tree's vigorous strength, which is consistent with the earlier image of the wild ox. The palm tree, in combination with the cedar of Lebanon, confirms the idea of strength that characterizes the righteous man who is immovable (see Ez 31:3-7), who is as sturdy as a ship's mast carved out of a cedar tree (Ez 27:25). The particular nature of these two trees comes from the location where they have been planted: they now adorn the court of the Temple. The message seems to be that only if the psalmist remains in the sphere of faith can he enjoy the nourishment the Lord gives and receive his stability.

vv. 14-15. Renewal of the invitation to acknowledge God's upright-ness. These two verses conclude the poem and, according to the literary genre of a hymn, should serve to reiterate the invitation to praise. Here the invitation is a bit obscure even though it is present. Verse 14 completes the vegetative cycle that began in verse 12 with the concept of flourishing because it mentions "fruit in old age" while again highlighting the vigor of the palm tree and the cedar that never diminishes. The invitation to praise, even though it is not conveyed directly as it usually is, is expressed by the infinitive verb "to show" in verse 15, because it creates a link to the infinitive verb "to declare" in verse 2 and refers to telling about God's qualities. At the end, the psalmist takes a clear stand: God is not responsible for the misfortune of the righteous or for the favor that the evil-doer seems to enjoy. The Lord is upright and demonstrates that by strengthening the just man, reviving his faith, bringing him into a vital relationship with himself, and freeing him from the shifting sands of unbelief. Therefore, YHWH is his rock (see 2 Sm 22:32; Ps 18:2; 31:3; 62:2,6; 144:1).

Psalm 103

A Psalm of David.

¹Bless the LORD, O my soul;
    and all that is within me, bless his holy name!
²Bless the LORD, O my soul,
    and forget not all his benefits,
³who forgives all your iniquity,
    who heals all your diseases,
⁴who redeems your life from the Pit,
    who crowns you with mercy and compassion,
⁵who satisfies you with good as long as you live
    so that your youth is renewed like the eagle's.

⁶The LORD works vindication
    and justice for all who are oppressed.
⁷He made known his ways to Moses,
    his acts to the people of Israel.
⁸The LORD is merciful and gracious,
    slow to anger and abounding in mercy.
⁹He will not always chide,
    nor will he keep his anger for ever.
¹⁰He does not deal with us according to our sins,
    nor repay us according to our iniquities.
¹¹For as the heavens are high above the earth,
    so great is his mercy toward those who fear him;

¹²as far as the east is from the west,
    so far does he remove our transgressions from us.
¹³ As a father pities his children,
    so the Lord pities those who fear him.
¹⁴For he knows our frame;
    he remembers that we are dust.
¹⁵As for man, his days are like grass;
    he flourishes like a flower of the field;
¹⁶for the wind passes over it, and it is gone,
    and its place knows it no more.
¹⁷But the mercy of the Lord is from everlasting to everlasting
    upon those who fear him,
    and his righteousness to children's children,
¹⁸to those who keep his covenant
    and remember to do his commandments.

¹⁹The Lord has established his throne in the heavens,
    and his kingdom rules over all.
²⁰Bless the Lord, O you his angels,
    you mighty ones who do his word,
    hearkening to the voice of his word!
²¹Bless the Lord, all his hosts,
    his ministers that do his will!
²² Bless the Lord, all his works,
    in all places of his dominion.
Bless the Lord, O my soul!

This is a hymn of praise that is tied to David, even though the heading does not specify any particular circumstance. The first verse is identical to the last verse, following a literary device called *inclusio* (also known as bracketing), which frames the psalm and gives a thematic unity to the benediction the psalmist is addressing to God. The blessing, characteristically offered by the soul and all its breath, begins and ends the poem (vv. 1a and 22b).

vv. 1-2. Initial call to the "whole" person. Earlier on we saw the word "soul" (*nephesh* in Hebrew), which, as already indicated, means "throat, breath, longing, desire." The second word we find in the Hebrew is "*qereb*," which is translated here as "all that is within me." *Qereb* in Hebrew means "innermost parts," or "entrails," and points to the deepest part of a human being. Starting with the first line of the psalm, there is an invitation to turn to God with all of one's strength and ability, reaching out to him energetically, literally, "with all of one's breath."

The phrase "forget not all his benefits" does not address a normal loss of memory, but evokes the theology of memory (*zikkaron*) that is so important in Jewish and Christian faiths. Not forgetting means having not just a psychological memory but a memory that is reactivated in the present so that the person recalling the events senses and participates in the reality of those events. For example, regarding the commandment for Passover, people are summoned to remember what happened in the past during the "now" of the ritual celebration (see Ex 12:14, and Jesus' statement in Lk 22:19 and 1 Cor 11:24: "Do this in remembrance of me").

vv. 3-10. Love instead of punishment. These verses comprise the first section of the psalm that celebrates love and forgiveness. The topic of sin appears at the beginning of this section in verse 3 and at the end in verse 10, framing the specific reasons for praising God.

Verses 3-4 tell us that the Lord forgives all "iniquity," which is the main reason he is being praised. What sin is the psalmist talking about? The word used in the original Hebrew is *'aon*, which refers to a multiplicity of misdeeds. They can be sins against God or against other people.

The second rationale for the man's praise is linked to the therapeutic character of the Lord who "heals all your diseases." There could be a dual reference here. In the Old Testament in particular there is a close connection between sin and physical sickness, so the Lord's forgiveness also confers physical health. We read in Psalm 51:8, "Make me hear joy and gladness: / let the bones which you have broken rejoice." A recovery of physical strength follows forgiveness and full reconciliation.

The second meaning of the statement derives from its link with verse 4, "who redeems your life from the Pit," which refers to God's intervention to rescue his faithful one from death. The pit recalls the tomb, the afterlife (*sheol*), pictured as a large hole that people sink down into (see Ps 7:15; 9:15; 16:10; 49:9; 94:13). Only YHWH can rescue people from the pit and allow them to return fully to life. Devout Jews are in fact concerned with the here and now because it is on earth that they experience God's goodness through his gifts of health and prosperity.

The second part of verse 4 mentions "mercy and compassion" (*hesed* and *rahamin*); the combination of those Hebrew words also appears in Psalm 23:6. These divine attributes describe two of God's qualities as well as his actions on behalf of his people, as we see in Exodus 34:6. Divine compassion (*rahamin*) involves visceral love, expressed as a profound, intense, maternal love (see Is 49:15). The overall image that emerges could be described as YHWH clasping the man to himself with his two arms of mercy and compassion, showering him with health and other benefits.

In verse 5, the recovery of health that comes along with forgiveness results in a prosperity that allows for a peaceful old age because it frees people from the anxiety of having to worry about material needs. According to the remunerative logic that links human righteousness to divine recompense, the psalmist is certain he will lack for nothing because the Lord will be taking care of him. He can enjoy having the things he needs precisely because he has been provided justice (see Ps 37:25: "I have been young, and now am old; / yet I have not seen the righteous forsaken / or his children begging bread.")

The image of the eagle in verse 5 evokes a picture of power, pride, and longevity. Perhaps the most evocative text to explain this symbol is in Deuteronomy 32:11-12:

Like an eagle that stirs up its nest,
    that flutters over its young,
spreading out its wings, catching them,
    bearing them on its pinions,
The LORD alone did lead him,
    and there was no foreign god with him.

The young psalmist is not afraid of old age, welcoming it as a growth in his understanding of faith and as a stage in which the good he has sowed throughout his life comes to fruition.

Divine protection in verse 6 involves defending the poor and oppressed. This is a very common theme in the preaching of the eighth-century prophets (Amos, Hosea, Isaiah, Jeremiah) who openly denounce worship that is disconnected from moral life. Isaiah 1:13 summarizes the sense of these prophetic warnings when the Lord says, "I cannot endure iniquity and solemn assembly." Psalm 58 also cries out against corrupt judges and calls for divine justice to intervene and reestablish the law. Judges have power over life and death, and that makes their function particularly significant. In the case of the chaste Susanna, for example, who was unjustly accused by two judges who wanted to take advantage of her, their false judgment against her could have led to her stoning or the loss of her freedom (see Dn 13). The psalmist is aware that only God is the defender of the weakest people, who in the biblical tradition are comprised of orphans, widows, and strangers (Dt 24:19-21).

In verses 7-10, we move from the personal level to the community level. This often happens in the psalms when the person who is praying weaves historical-salvific references in with his own circumstances. In verse 7, he evokes the event of the Exodus through the calling of Moses coupled with the history of the Israelite people. There are at least two other allusions here to events narrated in the Pentateuch. The first concerns assertions in verses 8 and 9 that have their basis in Exodus 34:6. Descriptions of God as "merciful" (*rahum*, from the same root as *rahamin*) and "gracious" (*chanan*) — also listed together in Psalm 86:5 — appear in the Exodus passage in which Moses asks to see God's glory: "And the LORD descended in the cloud and stood with him there, and proclaimed the name of the LORD. The LORD passed before him, and proclaimed, 'The LORD, the LORD, a God *merciful and gracious*, slow to anger, and abounding in mercy and faithfulness, keeping merciful love for thousands, forgiving iniquity and transgression and sin'" (Ex 34:5-7, emphasis added).

Verse 9 — "He will not always chide, / nor will he keep his anger for ever" — is also linked to another Moses event involving the dispute between Israel and YHWH at Meribah (see Ex 17), which causes Moses and his generation not to enter the Promised Land. (They are punished for having questioned the presence and power of God.) There is a final connection in this verse to the literary genre called *riv* in Hebrew, frequently translated as "controversy," a kind of legal debate between God and his people. Since the people of Israel failed to uphold their commitments in the covenant, God calls them to return to their responsibilities because he wants to reestablish the covenant relationship with his "partner." This psalm confirms that the Lord is not immovable in his judgments but is capable of becoming merciful because, as he says in Jeremiah, "I will not be angry for ever" (Jer 3:12).

The reference to sin that opened this section recurs in verse 10. The Lord goes beyond the "just rewards" approach of the traditional sin-punishment dynamic because he is aware of human weakness. Although he could assert his rights against Israel in a court of law, what moves him is not the desire to destroy his people but the desire to restore a relationship that was compromised by infidelity.

vv. 11-18. Second section: love vs. fragility. The cosmos becomes the backdrop for declaring the fullness and depth of God's love.

The vertical symbolism of heaven-earth in verse 11 is also recorded in Isaiah with the same intention of describing forgiveness:

"Seek the LORD while he may be found,
    call upon him while he is near;
let the wicked forsake his way,
    and the unrighteous man his thoughts;
let him return to the LORD, that he may have mercy on him,
    and to our God, for he will abundantly pardon.
For my thoughts are not your thoughts,
    neither are your ways my ways, says the LORD.
For as the heavens are higher than the earth,
    so are my ways higher than your ways
    and my thoughts than your thoughts. (Is 55:6-9)

The power of divine love, which is almost personified here, is extended to those who fear God. In the Bible's Wisdom literature, "fear of God" is the standard phrase to describe the attitude of affectionate thanksgiving and profound gratitude toward the One who is the source of all wisdom (see Prv 1:7; 2:6-7; 9:10; 15:33; 19:23; Sir 1:9; 19:20). According to the Psalter the fear of God dwells in the faithful — that is, God-fearing people — specifically those who participate in devout worship and lead irreproachable lives (Ps 22:23; 31:19; 66:16; 103:11,13,17). This ethical dimension becomes clear particularly in the texts that mention the Lord's covenant with his people (Ps 25:12,14; 34:9,11). One could say that there is a close identification between those who willingly follow the precepts of God's law and those who fear him.

Following this vertical symbolism, horizontal symbolism expresses the enormous distance between sin and the one who has committed it. It is the Lord who performs this separation and makes possible a release from the grip of sin. If sins are so oppressive that that they can suffocate people, the Lord intervenes and gives "new oxygen" to sinners, relieving them of their crushing burden of sin. However, this image of great distance can be applied to God as well. He is the one who distances himself from sin and casts it far behind him (see Is 38:17) or hurls it into the depths of the sea (Mi 7:19).

With recourse next to anthropological symbolism in verse 13 and 14, the psalmist presents one of the most beautiful images in the poem: God as Father. The text that can best comment on these verses is from Hosea 11:

> When Israel was a child, I loved him,
>   and out of Egypt I called my son.
> The more I called them,
>   the more they went from me;
> they kept sacrificing to the Baals,
>   and burning incense to idols.
>
> Yet it was I who taught Ephraim to walk,
>   I took them up in my arms;
>   but they did not know that I healed them.
> I led them with cords of compassion,
>   with the bands of love,
> and I became to them as one
>   who raises an infant to his cheeks,
>   and I bent down to them and fed them.
>
> I will not execute my fierce anger,
>   I will not again destroy Ephraim;
> for I am God and not man,
>   the Holy One in your midst,
>   and I will not come to destroy." (vv. 1-4,9)

On this topic, Psalm 27:10 states that even if parents forsake their children, the Lord will never forget Israel. Even though we generally think that God's fatherhood is a revelation exclusive to the New Testament, these passages demonstrate that even in the Old Covenant God is thought of in affectionate family terms.

What propels God to mercy is his awareness of the spiritual poverty of the human condition. Precisely because he knows the innermost workings of human beings, he considers the totality of their fallenness (see Gn 3:8-19). Even though human beings are created in his image and likeness, they are still the dust of the earth, according to the pun in Genesis where Adam is taken from *adamah*, from the earth, to which he will return. God's forbearance, then, is on a par with his profound understanding of human nature. Psalm 78:39 speaks of God's mercy as motivated by his awareness that human beings are "but flesh."

Back to Psalm 103, the word used in verse 15 for man is the Hebrew *enosh*, and it emphasizes precisely this fallenness, precariousness, and fragility.

Verses 15 to 16 develop the idea of precariousness with the image of grass and the flowers of the field that are at the mercy of the wind. They cannot put up any resistance because they are constitutionally fragile. A lovely text from the Book of Sirach (c. 180 B.C.) wonderfully describes this condition:

> What is man, and of what use is he?
>> What is his good and what is his evil?
> The number of a man's days is great if he reaches
>> a hundred years.
> Like a drop of water from the sea and a grain of sand
>> so are a few years in the day of eternity.
> Therefore the Lord is patient with them
>> and pours out his mercy upon them.
> He sees and recognizes that their end will be evil;
>> therefore he grants them forgiveness in abundance.
>> (18:8-12)

Turning to the New Testament, how can we not consider Jesus' cry on the cross — "Father, forgive them; for they know not what they do" (Lk 23:34) — as the ultimate proof of his love, a love that makes him consider the worst crime by humanity as a desperate act of people's ignorance?

The word "mercy" (*hesed*) is repeated in verse 17. If the grass and flowers represent people's brief sojourn on earth, then God's throne, established in the heavens, represents the perennial nature of his love-mercy (see v. 19). The psalmist is explicit in insisting on its perennial nature, saying his mercy "is from everlasting to everlasting." His justice is understood in the sense of a desire to care for the oppressed and the "children's children," an expression meaning "for all generations."

Who are the recipients of his abundant love? Those who fear God, the righteous, those who keep the covenant and observe its commandments. Mention of the covenant and commandments reverts to the context of Sinai, the Decalogue, and God's theophany: "Now therefore, if you will obey my voice and keep my covenant, you shall be my own possession among all peoples; for all the earth is mine, and you shall be to me a kingdom of priests and a holy nation" (Ex 19:5-6). To be his "possession among all peoples" (*segullah*) means entering into a unique relationship with God that includes a powerful connection to his care and protection. The psalmist's hymn is thus enriched by the fundamental elements that nourish the Jewish faith in his declaration of the universal lordship of YHWH in verse 19.

vv. 20–22. Final benediction. This benediction calls on the whole celestial court, pictured as a large crowd of angelic figures who are in total service to God (see Is 6:1-3). Although the expression "Lord of hosts" (*YHWH tzava'ot*) is generally understood as a warlike expression because it also means "Lord of armies," a different connotation of peace and love emerges in the theology of this psalm. God wants to be feared for his benevolence, not for tyrannical reasons:

> For it is always in your power to show great strength,
> and who can withstand the might of your arm?
> Because the whole world before you is like a speck that
>   tips the scales,
> and like a drop of morning dew that falls upon the ground.

But you are merciful to all, for you can do all things,
and you overlook men's sins, that they may repent.
For you love all things that exist,
and you loathe none of the things which you have made,
for you would not have made anything if you had hated it.
How would anything have endured if you had not willed it?
Or how would anything not called forth by you have been
      preserved?
You spare all things, for they are yours, O Lord who love the
      living. (Wis 11:21-26)

The refrain "Bless the LORD, O my soul (*nephesh*)" ends the poem that begins with this very statement. The framing of the poem this way expresses the perennial nature of praise that the psalmist is called to and that will have no end.

Psalm 119:81-88

⁸¹My soul languishes for your salvation;
    I hope in your word.
⁸²My eyes fail with watching for your promise;
    I ask, "When will you comfort me?"
⁸³For I have become like a wineskin in the smoke,
    yet I have not forgotten your statutes.
⁸⁴How long must your servant endure?
    When will you judge those who persecute me?
⁸⁵Godless men have dug pitfalls for me,
    men who do not conform to your law.
⁸⁶All your commandments are sure;
    they persecute me with falsehood; help me!
⁸⁷They have almost made an end of me on earth;
    but I have not forsaken your precepts.
⁸⁸In your mercy spare my life,
    that I may keep the testimonies of your mouth.

Psalm 119 is the longest psalm in the Psalter. It follows the alphabetical procedure we saw in Psalm 25, but with a major difference. In Psalm 25, every verse begins with an alphabetical letter, but in Psalm 119, every one of the twenty-two stanzas begins with an alphabetical letter. The rationale for this structure is always a desire to offer a comprehensive prayer — from "A" to "Z." In this case it involves the desire to incorporate all that could be said about the topic of the Law (the Torah). The Torah is, in fact, at the center of this meditation that presents lengthy praise for the richness and power of the Word of God.

As the basis for our reflection, let us look at the stanza that is designated for the letter *Kaph* (our letter "k" and the eleventh letter of the Hebrew alphabet), in which the word "mercy" appears (see v. 88). The poem is set out as a lamentation that is very close to the Wisdom tradition because it includes the theme of persecution by one's enemies (vv. 84-86).

v. 81. The "k" word that begins this section of the psalm, *Kalah*, appears in verses 81, 82, and 87. It means, "to languish, to fail, to be consumed," and also, as in verse 87, "to be destroyed." The first two verses describe the psychological situation of the man who is praying. They tell of his deep torment linked to his waiting for the Lord's salvation. He does not specify the reason for his suffering. From the description of his enemies, it seems they are godless men who lash out against whoever desires to live according to his religious beliefs. It could be he also finds himself being unjustly accused and is confidently awaiting God's judgment so that justice will be restored (see v. 84). The psalmist is now at the end of his rope and is hoping for speedy intervention by God in one of his decisive judgments. The word *nephesh*, which we already encountered in other psalms, appears in verse 81 and expresses his longing with a deep sigh: when someone says *nephesh* out loud, its pronunciation requires the act of inhaling and exhaling.

v. 82. The second occurrence of the verb *Kalah* is less psychological and refers to his dried, dehydrated eyes. The cause of this condition could be twofold. The first cause of his eye dryness could derive from prolonged weeping because of an illness. We read in Psalm 31:

> my eye is wasted from grief,
>   my soul and my body also.
> For my life is spent with sorrow,
>   and my years with sighing;

my strength fails because of my misery,
> and my bones waste away. (vv. 9-10)

A very similar description occurs in Psalm 6:

I am weary with my moaning;
> every night I flood my bed with tears;
> I drench my couch with my weeping.
My eye wastes away because of grief,
> it grows weak because of all my foes. (vv. 6-7)

An eye that is wasting away can be a symptom of approaching death, an eye that is in bad condition or almost blind; at the opposite pole, light in one's eyes is a sign of vigorous life (see Ps 19:8).

A second cause for his dehydrated eyes is weeping because of the unbelief of others. That reason is particularly relevant to this stanza because it is found in another passage in this psalm: "My eyes shed streams of tears, / because men do not keep your law" (v. 136). Despite the possibility of a medical condition affecting his eyes, his weeping here seems due to the persecution of unbelieving people who make the life of a person of faith unbearable.

v. 83. The image of a wineskin exposed to smoke has the effect of continuing the theme of weeping, because smoke in one's eyes causes burning and painful tearing. The man who is praying is continuously exposed to the oppression of his enemies who make his life intolerable to the point of stifling him. Another meaning of "wineskin in the smoke" could be linked to old age. Just as a leather bag can be blackened by continued exposure to smoke, so, too, the psalmist could be declaring his aging or darkening. In Lamentations 4:8, we read, "Now their visage is blacker than soot, / they are not recognized in the streets; / their skin has shriveled upon their bones, / it has become dry as wood." What gives this man his strength are the precepts of the Lord that he vividly remembers: "I have not forgotten your statutes" (v. 83).

v. 84. According to the style of a lamentation, the psalmist asks God two questions that could be rephrased this way: How long will God's silence last? And when will his judgment come? What causes the man's suffering is not only his objective situation, but also the subjective situation of someone whose intense, prolonged suffering causes him to wonder about God's justice. We already recalled Job's situation and his protest against God's silence in our commentary on Psalm 42. We can also notice here that the allusion to a court tribunal is especially similar to the event in Job in which the protagonist accuses God of injustice. Here, the psalmist hopes to receive justice from God, the righteous judge.

v. 85. A pit is a symbol of death and of the entrance to the underworld. The psalmist alludes here to the fact that only YHWH can rescue someone from the devouring pit of the afterlife (see Ps 9:13; 16:10; 49:15; 94:17).

There are two possible profiles for his persecutors. The first lists traits of people who go after other people for the sole reason that they are believers. Chapter 2 of the Wisdom of Solomon describes the hostile attitude of the ungodly (Greek, *asebēs*, "impious") toward the righteous person. The wicked decide to do him harm because his presence and his lifestyle bother them: "Let us lie in wait for the righteous man, / because he is inconvenient to us and opposes our actions; / he reproaches us for sins against the law, / and accuses us of sins against our training" (v. 12). The psalmist's special and intimate relationship with God is perceived as a threat:

> He professes to have knowledge of God,
> and calls himself a child of the Lord.
> He became to us a reproof of our thoughts;
> the very sight of him is a burden to us.
> We are considered by him as something base,
> and he avoids our ways as unclean;
> he calls the last end of the righteous happy,
> and boasts that God is his father. (Wis 2:13-15a,16)

His life lies outside of the usual standards of behavior: "His manner of life is unlike that of others, / and his ways are strange" (2:15b). The decision to test the man's integrity takes on the tone of a challenge to everything he represents:

> Let us see if his words are true,
> and let us test what will happen at the end of his life;
> for if the righteous man is God's son, he will help him,
> and will deliver him from the hand of his adversaries.
> Let us test him with insult and torture,
> that we may find out how gentle he is,
> and make trial of his forbearance. (2:17-19)

The psalmist wants to attain his goal of receiving validation and confirmation for his way of life, which is discounted by the evildoers: "Let us condemn him to a shameful death, / for, according to what he says, he will be protected" (Wis 2:20). These words from Wisdom and Psalm 119 apply to religious persecutions in every age. However, in a particular and unique way, they recall the life of Jesus, the righteous man par excellence, who was oppressed, mocked, and killed by evildoers (see Mt 27:1-50; Mk 15:16-37).

vv. 86-87. The more the hostility of the persecutors rages, the more the psalmist proclaims his faith and his unbounded trust in God and in his Word. "God's Word" here refers to his commandments or teachings (Torah) and precepts (*mitzvot*), which in the Pentateuch tradition refer both to statutes and to the revealed Word (see Dt 6).

The psalmist aligns himself with the heart of Israel's faith as the rationale for his choices. He links the indicative verb of his will — "I have not forsaken your precepts" (v. 87) — to the primary imperative command of faith, "Hear O Israel . . . " (Dt 6:4), thus strengthening his relationship with the Lord. In the First Letter of Peter there is a passage that expresses this situation of fruitfulness in times of adversity very clearly: "In this you rejoice, though now for a little while you may have to suffer various trials, so that the genuineness of your faith, more precious than gold which though perishable is tested by fire, may redound to praise and glory and honor at the revelation of Jesus Christ. Without having seen him you love him; though you do not now see him you believe in him and rejoice with unutterable and exalted joy. As the outcome of your faith you obtain the salvation of your souls" (1:6-9). The recipients of Peter's letter are being persecuted for the simple fact of professing their faith in Christ, and the apostle exhorts them to persevere because there is a mysterious fruit that this hostility brings with it.

v. 88. There is no spirit of vengeance in the psalmist's words. He does not desire the death of his enemy nor does he hope for the law of retaliation — "eye for eye, tooth for tooth" (Ex 21:24; Lev 24:20; Dt 19:21) — as he could have legitimately done. When he says, "In your mercy [*hesed*] spare my life," there are two complementary ways this can be understood. Because the Hebrew particle *ke* means "according to" (translated here as "in"), the one praying is opening himself up to the gift that comes from God, the gift of a full, rich life that is "according to," meaning "in proportion to," his mercy. In addition, "according to your mercy" can have a motivational value that could be phrased this way: "Because of your love, spare my life." In other words, in the first interpretation the psalmist hopes for a full, long life according to God's measure — and God's measure would be "without measure." In the second interpretation the emphasis is on the dynamic linked to the grace of merciful love and its consequences day after day: "Because of your love I can live."

Psalm 136

¹O give thanks to the Lord, for he is good,
    for his mercy endures for ever.
²O give thanks to the God of gods,
    for his mercy endures for ever.
³O give thanks to the Lord of lords,
    for his mercy endures for ever;

⁴to him who alone does great wonders,
    for his mercy endures for ever;
⁵to him who by understanding made the heavens,
    for his mercy endures for ever;
⁶to him who spread out the earth upon the waters,
    for his mercy endures for ever;
⁷to him who made the great lights,
    for his mercy endures for ever;
⁸the sun to rule over the day,
    for his mercy endures for ever;
⁹the moon and stars to rule over the night,
    for his mercy endures for ever;

¹⁰to him who smote the first-born of Egypt,
    for his mercy endures for ever;
¹¹and brought Israel out from among them,
    for his mercy endures for ever;

[12]with a strong hand and an outstretched arm,
    for his mercy endures for ever;
[13]to him who divided the Red Sea in two,
    for his mercy endures for ever;
[14]and made Israel pass through the midst of it,
    for his mercy endures for ever;
[15]but overthrew Pharaoh and his host in
        the Red Sea,
    for his mercy endures for ever;
[16]to him who led his people through the wilderness,
    for his mercy endures for ever;
[17]to him who struck great kings,
    for his mercy endures for ever;
[18]and slew famous kings,
    for his mercy endures for ever;
[19]Sihon, king of the Amorites,
    for his mercy endures for ever;
[20]and Og, king of Bashan,
    for his mercy endures for ever;
[21]and gave their land as a heritage,
    for his mercy endures for ever;
[22]a heritage to Israel his servant,
    for his mercy endures for ever.

[23]It is he who remembered us in our low estate,
    for his mercy endures for ever;
[24]and rescued us from our foes,
    for his mercy endures for ever;
[25]he who gives food to all flesh,
    for his mercy endures for ever.

[26]O give thanks to the God of heaven,
    for his mercy endures for ever.

This psalm is a thanksgiving hymn par excellence and is used during the Passover, the Feast of Tabernacles, and Rosh Hashanah. It has a lyrical rhythm because of the refrain "for his mercy endures forever," which is repeated for every event in the history of salvation (creation, redemption, the gift of land). This psalm is also called "the Great Hallel" (from the verb *halah*, "to praise," which also gives us the word "alleluia"). The psalm is a good representation of the theme of spiritual maturity that characterizes the fifth book of the Psalter. As Pope Francis says in the bull of indiction of the extraordinary Jubilee of Mercy, *Misericordiae Vultus*:

> Before his passion, Jesus prayed this psalm of mercy. Matthew attests to this in his Gospel when he says that, "when they had sung a hymn" (Mt 26:30), Jesus and his disciples went out to the Mount of Olives. While he was instituting the Eucharist as an everlasting memorial of himself and his paschal sacrifice, he symbolically placed this supreme act of revelation in the light of his mercy. Within the very same context of mercy, Jesus entered upon his passion and death, conscious of the great mystery of love that he would consummate on the Cross. Knowing that Jesus himself prayed this psalm makes it even more important for us as Christians, challenging us to take up the refrain in our daily lives by praying these words of praise: "for his mercy endures forever." (7)

After the first three verses that invite us to grateful praise in this psalm, there comes the record of creation (see vv. 4-9), the deliverance from Egypt with the miracles that accompanied it (vv. 10-16), and the destruction of Israel's enemies (vv. 17-22). The last four verses summarize the benefits being received now, including food. The first and last verses form an *inclusio*, a framing of the poem into a literary unity because these verses are practically the same.

vv. 1–3. Invitation to praise. There is no title for the psalm. We could consider the first three verses as a heading that points to the psalm's theme: thanksgiving for the goodness and mercy of the Lord (see v. 1), who has absolute superiority over other gods (v. 2) and absolute sovereignty over the rulers of the earth (v. 3). In Deuteronomy 10:17, a passage which praises God's action on behalf of his people and especially the poor, two titles of God are recorded together the same way they are here: "For the LORD your God is *God of gods* and *Lord of lords*, the great, the mighty, and the terrible God, who is not partial and takes no bribes" (emphasis added).

The word *hesed* ("mercy" or "steadfast love") is repeated twenty-six times, occurring in every verse according to the rhythm of the poem. All of the history of salvation is reviewed from the perspective of God's mercy and his loving determination to intervene on behalf of his people from the beginning of creation until now. The words "for ever" express the unchangeable nature of such a love that will never end and will never decrease. The goal of the remembrance and re-elaboration of the past is to demonstrate God's actions on behalf of his people, resulting in a lesson in faith and hope for the present-day community. St. John Paul II, commenting on the psalmist's awareness of God's love, said: "By being vitally immersed in the Hebrew tradition of prayer, Christians learned to pray by recounting the *magnalia Dei,* that is, the great marvels worked by God both in the creation of the world and humanity, and in the history of Israel and the Church.... [For this reason] the Book of Psalms remains the ideal source of Christian prayer" (General Audience, March 28, 2001).

vv. 4–9. Creation. Specific knowledge of creation, although it had always been part of Israel's creed, became more explicit during the Babylonian Exile (597-538 B.C.), so this could be a minor clue for a possible dating of this psalm.

The verb *'asah,* which means "to mold, to shape," appears three times in the account of creation (see vv. 4, 5, 7) to convey the picture of a Creator-God who is close to his creatures and "forges" things with his own hands the way a potter does with clay. In just a few verses, all of creation's constitutive elements are mentioned: heaven, earth, water, sun, and moon. In Genesis 1:6, God creates heaven (*shamayim* is actually a plural) and separates the waters under the firmament from the waters above it. The firmament (*raqia'*) is depicted as a canopy of beaten metal whose purpose is to hold back the force of the waters above and the waters below. In verse 5, the heavens are created through "understanding" or wisdom, similar to what Proverbs says of the mediation of Wisdom:

> When he established the heavens, I [Wisdom] was there,
>> when he drew a circle on the face of the deep,
> when he made firm the skies above,
>> when he established the fountains of the deep,
> when he assigned to the sea its limit,
>> so that the waters might not transgress his command,
> when he marked out the foundations of the earth,
>> then I was beside him, like a master workman;
> and I was daily his delight,
>> rejoicing before him always. (Prv 8:27-30)

God's work is the result of his will to create an orderly and harmonious world, a habitat adapted for human life as we see in Genesis 1-2.

In verses 6-9, the earth (*'eretz*) is pictured as laid out over the waters according to Genesis 1:9-10; God channels the waters for dry land to emerge and float on the sea. The sun and the moon in Genesis 1:16 are called "the two great lights"; according to the theological perspective of the author, these heavenly bodies are simply signs to regulate the calendar for feasts and seasons. He presented them this way to avoid leaving any room whatsoever for the astral divinities that were worshiped in neighboring nations. The names of these astral bodies (sun, moon, stars) appear with no implied concern for idolatry because everything is explicitly linked back to

God's omnipotence that rules everything. In Psalm 136, as is the case in Genesis, the astral bodies are ascribed the regulatory function of illuminating the earth.

vv. 10-16. Deliverance from Egypt. Events narrated in Exodus and Numbers are recalled in verses 10-22 and constitute the major part of the psalm. This next section could be considered answers to the question, "When did Israel experience divine mercy?" Israel experienced mercy when it was in difficulty, when it was enslaved and oppressed, and when it was journeying in the desert. The psalm recounts the tenth plague, the death of the first-born, which is particularly tied to the rite of Passover (see Ex 12). The Lord asked that blood from the Passover sacrificial lamb be sprinkled on the lintels of the doorposts as the sign of an Israelite dwelling. God's right hand represents his saving power, as in the passage through the Red Sea (Ex 15:6); his actions are described in terms of having "brought Israel out" (v. 11), a verb to indicate the Exodus that implies engineering ability (Nm 20:16; Dt 6:21). In verses 13-15, events occurring at the Red Sea are described in basic detail: Israel's passage through the sea and the deaths of Pharaoh and his army when the waters closed in over them at Moses' command (Ex 14).

The theme of the wilderness appears in verse 16. The prophetic tradition often mentions the wilderness or the desert more as a season of time than as a place. During the forty years in the desert, YHWH was Israel's only security, but during the time of their establishment in the Promised Land the people lived a kind of sedentary life spiritually, forgetting God's benefits and his watching over them. In the eighth century B.C., Hosea, the prophet of love par excellence, refers to a time in the desert, associating it to a time of falling in love. (Israel here is described as Gomer, the prophet's unfaithful spouse.) The goal of being in the "desert" is to rekindle Israel's love, a love that is now tepid and even marred by infidelity:

> "And in that day, says the LORD, you will call me, 'My husband,' and no longer will you call me, 'My Baal.' And

I will make for you a covenant on that day with the beasts of the field, the birds of the air, and the creeping things of the ground; and I will abolish the bow, the sword, and war from the land; and I will make you lie down in safety.

"And in that day, says the LORD,

> I will answer the heavens
> and they shall answer the earth;
> and the earth shall answer the grain, the wine,
> and the oil,
> and they shall answer Jezreel,"
>
> (Hos 2:16,18,21-22)

The mercy of the Lord is demonstrated in the loving care that Israel received in terms of guidance, food, and clothing, as we read in the Book of Deuteronomy: "I have led you forty years in the wilderness; your clothes have not worn out upon you, and your sandals have not worn off your feet; you have not eaten bread, and you have not drunk wine or strong drink; that you may know that I am the LORD your God" (29:5-6).

vv. 17-22. Destruction of Israel's enemies. Another sign of divine protection occurs in connection to the tyranny of nations and their leaders with whom Israel clashed (see Nm 21:21-35; Dt 3:1-11; Jos 2:10). Two kings are named in this psalm, Sihon and Og, also mentioned in Deuteronomy 1:4 and Psalm 135:11, with the purpose of inspiring the people to righteous observance of God's precepts: "And when you came to this place, Sihon the king of Heshbon and Og the king of Bashan came out against us to battle, but we defeated them; we took their land, and gave it for an inheritance to the Reubenites, the Gadites, and the half-tribe of the Manassites. Therefore be careful to do the words of this covenant, that you may prosper in all you do" (Dt 29:7-9).

Aside from the historical and geographical connotations, the psalmist wants to emphasize God's power against all the enemies of his people. The pagan nations (*goyim*) are presented briefly as the symbol of wicked people and enemies of Israel. A more standard list of enemy names, which is almost always identical, appears in some other Old Testament texts: Canaanites, Hittites, Amorites, Perizzites, Hivites, and Jebusites. The two kings mentioned in this psalm, Sihon and Og, are considered the leaders of the adversaries that YHWH destroyed to make room for his elect.

vv. 23-26. Remembering past benefits and listing present benefits. The topic of the people's "low estate" in verse 23 can refer to all the situations in which Israel experienced humiliation because of so many infidelities (see 1 Kgs 8:35). But it is the Babylonian Exile in particular, with the consequent loss of the Promised Land and Temple worship, that represents the lowest point of Israel's history because it created consternation, disorientation, and confusion:

> *"For we, O Lord, have become fewer than any nation,*
>   *and are brought low this day in all the world because of our sins.*
> *And at this time there is no prince, or prophet, or leader,*
>   *no burnt offering, or sacrifice, or oblation, or incense,*
>   *no place to make an offering before you or to find mercy.*
> *Yet with a contrite heart and a humble spirit may we be accepted,*
>   *as though it were with burnt offerings of rams and bulls,*
>   *and with tens of thousands of fat lambs."* (Dn 3:14-16)

In defeating Israel's historical adversaries, the Lord demonstrates his faithfulness to the promise given to Abraham (see Lk 1:54-55; also see Gn 12:1-7: "He helped his servant Israel / in remembrance of his mercy / as he spoke to our fathers, / to Abraham and to his posterity forever").

Verse 25 records an image, which is widespread throughout the Psalms, of God giving food to every living thing (see Ps 104:27-28; 145:15-16; 147:9; Acts 14:17). When the Hebrew speaks of "all flesh," it broadens the horizon of God's mercy to all creatures and thus includes the animals as well. We see the same concept in Psalm 36:6: "Your righteousness is like the mountains of God, / your judgments are like the great deep; / man and beast you save, O Lord."

Verse 26 ends the poem, echoing its first verse. According to Gianfranco Ravasi, the credo finishes here, but it is not ended because it reverts to the beginning in a kind of perennial loop of praise: God will never cease loving, saving, and giving, and therefore our thanksgiving can never stop.[3] Mercy — not hate, vengeance, injustice, and abuse of power — is the key to reading history. Mercy enables us to avoid narrowing our perspective to the presence of any given temporary conflict because it breaks the cycle of the law of retaliation, moving history and humanity's path forward to their fulfillment in God.

---

3. See Gianfranco Ravasi, *Il Libro dei Salmi*, vol. 3 (Bolgona: Edizioni Dehoniane Bologna, 2008), 742.